Margot Northey
Queen's University
Margaret Procter
University of Toronto

Writer's Choice

A Portable Guide for Canadian Writers

Vincent Cooney
Victoria Hall
'D' Wing
Room 613
(613) 533-8521
Kingston, On

Prentice Hall Canada Inc.,
Scarborough, Ontario

Canadian Cataloguing in Publication Data

Northey, Margot, 1940-
Writer's choice : a portable guide for Canadian students

Includes index.
ISBN 0-13-736208-0

1. Exposition (Rhetoric). 2. English language - Rhetoric.
I. Procter, Margaret, 1944- . II. Title.

LB2369.N677 1998 808'.042 C97-930526-8

Prentice-Hall, Inc., Upper Saddle River, New Jersey
Prentice-Hall International (UK) Limited, London
Prentice-Hall of Australia, Pty. Limited, Sydney
Prentice-Hall Hispanoamericana, S.A., Mexico City
Prentice-Hall of India Private Limited, New Delhi
Prentice-Hall of Japan, Inc., Tokyo
Simon & Schuster Southeast Asia Private Limited, Singapore
Editora Prentice-Hall do Brasil, Ltda., Rio de Janeiro

ISBN 0-13-736208-0

Vice President, Editorial Director: Laura Pearson
Acquisitions Editor: Rebecca Bersagel
Developmental Editor: Lisa Berland
Production Editor: Amber Wallace
Copy Editor: Rodney Rawlings
Production Coordinator: Jane Schell
Permissions: Marijke Leupen
Cover/Interior Design: Monica Kompter
Page Layout: B.J. Weckerle

5 BB 03 02

Printed and bound in Canada

TABLE OF CONTENTS

PREFACE

This handbook will provide you with a reliable and up-to-date reference guide to writing, whatever your field of study—humanities, social science, science, business, or a profession. We designed it to be accessible, so you can easily find the information you want and use it in the different situations you meet.

Writer's Choice is genuinely *A Portable Guide for Canadian Students*. It's selective and concise, so that you can carry it around from one class to another and have it on hand whenever you need to look something up. It concentrates on topics that students say they want to be informed about, with attention to common problem areas. The choice of material reflects a research survey we conducted at several colleges and universities, exploring student writing needs and difficulties. It also reflects our extensive experience teaching a wide range of students.

By reading this book and looking up answers to your questions, you will learn not only how to connect with your reader and put your ideas into coherent prose, but also how to apply ideas about writing to your own needs. The book will help you become a more confident and competent writer in all the subjects you take and in your future work. You can use this book in several ways:

1. ***For extensive guidance on a broad area***, such as organizing an essay or reviewing grammar, turn to the appropriate chapter (for instance, *The Essay* or *Standard Grammar*) and read the relevant section.

2. ***To find out about a specific smaller point***, such as verb tense, turn to the index at the back and find the pages where it is discussed.

3. ***For more guidance on key topics***, follow up the numerous cross-references we have provided. These cross-references eliminate repetition and keep this handbook lean.

The advice we offer in *Writer's Choice* addresses the current realities of writing in our complex world. The icons shown below mark places where we discuss four important aspects of language use.

- ***Technology.*** Computers have changed the process of creating written documents. This book reflects the growing role of word processing, e-mail, electronic reference resources, and research databases, and it offers advice on using them effectively.

- ***Language trends.*** Language changes over the years, and it changes especially fast when many people are communicating rapidly. We note a variety of trends in the ways people write, including preferences in vocabulary and punctuation, and changes in patterns of organizing documents. Our discussion will help you make choices.

- ***International differences.*** In this era of expanding internationalism, writers need to recognize that patterns of written English differ from one country to another. *Writer's Choice* points out the areas where Canadians can choose among different traditions.

- ***English as a second language.*** Because we live in what Marshall McLuhan called "a global village," many Canadians use English in addition to their mother tongue. Our discussion of usage acknowledges the special questions and concerns of people learning English as a second language.

Writer's Choice emphasizes guidelines more than rules, since written English takes so many forms. You will need to make choices based on context—the purpose of your writing, the preferences of your readers, and the conventions of your subjects. We help you see exactly what the choices are.

We welcome feedback on this book. We hope you will enjoy using it, not just for your present writing assignments but also as a handy reference guide for years to come.

Margot Northey and Margaret Procter

ACKNOWLEDGEMENTS

Many people have helped us in preparing this handbook. We thank our colleague Susan Watt of Sheridan College for helping us gather data on what students see as problems in their writing tasks.

We also owe gratitude to our colleagues at the University of Toronto for their insights and encouragement over the years, and to our students there and elsewhere for their stimulating questions and patience in waiting for answers. We thank especially Marjatta Holt of the University of Toronto for showing that second-language problems can be explained intelligibly. Alison Sills and Andrea Procter contributed their essays as samples, and they and Ken Sills scrutinized our prose for places to laugh at. Crystal Fulton receives our thanks for helping find examples for the grammar and punctuation sections. Our friend Pam Young efficiently brought scattered bits and pieces together for a number of sections, and Rebecca Cameron wielded the word processor and her keen good sense to put things into final form. We thank the following reviewers who gave us good advice at the final-draft stage: Jim Bell, University of Northern British Columbia; Ann Boyd, Ryerson Polytechnic University; Barb Christian, University of Guelph; Betty Holmes, Seneca College; and Vappu Tyyska, University of Toronto. And we are grateful to our editors at Prentice Hall, Rebecca Bersagel and Lisa Berland, for their continuous encouragement and wise advice. The last word of thanks must go to Rodney Rawlings, who demonstrated the value of careful copy-editing.

CHAPTER 1

THE WRITING PROCESS: Making Effective Choices

Academic writing isn't easy, but it can be rewarding. Like any other worthwhile activity, from music to sports, it requires practice and an understanding of what you're doing. You can make the challenge more manageable—and more satisfying—by thinking of it as a process with several parts. It includes a number of planning, drafting, and editing stages, and various chances to consider readers' responses. Depending on the type of assignments you face and your experience and skill, some of these activities will take more time and effort than others.

Along the way you will make many choices, usually not between right and wrong ways of doing things, but between what is more effective or less effective for your task. This chapter provides guidelines to help you make wise choices. After working through various kinds of assignments and assessing the results, you will become confident about applying our advice to various kinds of writing and adapting it for your own purposes.

Planning

Planning a writing task can't be rushed. It requires time—time to question, time to consider, and time to sort out the issues that always arise from exploring a topic intelligently. Most writing assignments ask you to think deeply and clearly about the topics even before you begin to write.

Thinking Through the Task

Before you start writing, spend time analyzing what you are going to do. Read the assignment sheet carefully, and look for key words to help answer these questions:

1. What Is the Purpose?

Are you setting out to gather information about a topic? To explore the range of opinions on a topic? To show that you understand a concept or theory? To argue or defend a point of view? To try to solve a problem? Each goal suggests a different approach to thinking and writing.

For example, if you are exploring a topic, you may raise questions and uncover issues, whereas in a problem-solving assignment you will move toward recommendations for action. If your purpose is to show that you understand a theory, you will probably need to summarize the theory succinctly and set out examples of how it works in practice. If your purpose is to defend a point of view, you will have to pay special attention to the logic of your reasoning and the evidence supporting your case.

2. Who Is the Reader?

The reader for an academic assignment is nearly always your instructor, a specialist in the subject you're writing about. That means, first of all, that you don't need to repeat information the instructor has discussed

PRACTICAL TIP

Understanding the Assignment

Studying the verbs on an assignment sheet is the shortest way to understand "what the instructor wants." The most common verbs ask you to display your powers of reasoning, not just collect facts or show you have read a text. With experience, you will recognize the intended task, even if different words are used. (And you can always ask your instructor for further guidance on this crucial step.)

- **Analyze** means look behind the surface structure of your source material—break it up and see the relationship of parts to whole. Be able to recognize connections such as cause and effect. Look for underlying assumptions and question their validity. *How* and *why* imply an answer reached by analysis.
- **Compare** means find differences as well as similarities. Decide what aspects you will look at in each item, and try organizing your discussion to look at each aspect in turn.
- **Evaluate** means apply your judgement to the results of your analysis or comparison. Formulate an opinion based on well-defined standards and clearly stated evidence. Wording such as *to what extent* also asks you to evaluate an idea.
- **Argue** (or **agree or disagree**) means analyze a controversial topic, compare different views, and put forward your own preferred view. Provide solid evidence to show why your view is preferable, but remain respectful of the others.
- **Discuss** is similar to argue, but usually broader. It means set out all sides in an argument, treating each fairly. Give only enough factual information to set the topic in context; show how it can be seen from different viewpoints.

in class or already knows. For example, don't summarize a given reading unless specifically asked to. Instead, analyze it, advancing the discussion begun in class.

Keep in mind that the reader will assess what you say within the framework of a particular subject area or discipline. That's not to say you should "play up to the teacher." But don't be shy about using concepts and methods of analysis taught in your course. In literary studies, for instance, you would be given credit for distinguishing between reliable and unreliable narrators, while for anthropology you might gain depth by trying a structuralist approach to an Ojibwa ceremony you've read about. Be sure, of course, that you understand the concepts accurately and that they fit your examples.

3. What Are the Time Frame, the Length, and the Expected Scope?

Student writers often try to cover too broad a territory without enough depth to satisfy the reader or themselves. Recognizing how much time and space you have will help you develop ideas adequately. You are usually allowed—even encouraged—to narrow topics so that you can do a good job.

If you are uncertain about answering these questions, or about any other aspect of the assignment itself, check with your instructor before you plunge ahead.

Searching for Ideas

Whether you have an assigned topic or an open one, you have a subject to develop. You will need to gather information and find out what other people have thought, but more important, you will deepen your own thinking. You'll develop the ability to think critically: to analyze various points of view, compare interpretations, and explore beneath the surface of common assumptions. You'll apply those operations to what you read as well as to your own writing.

1. Ask Yourself What Ideas You're Starting With

Learning starts with who you are and what you think already. And to achieve objectivity, you need to see what framework you're starting from.

- ***What do you know about the subject?*** Before you do any reading or writing, jot down a list of the facts you know about the topic. You'll probably notice some gaps, and you may even realize that your knowledge is based on unreliable sources such as hearsay or childhood teaching.
- ***What are your preliminary opinions?*** It's important to recognize your own attitude to the topic, especially if you intend to argue a position. Try writing your present opinion in one sentence ending with one or two *because* clauses: "I support free trade with Chile because it will bring prosperity to both countries and because it will encourage democratization." Now you have reminded yourself to examine the evidence for those *because* statements, and to consider whether they really support your opinion.

2. Explore the Possibilities of the Topic Through Freewriting

Professional writers use a variety of techniques to start ideas flowing.* You may be able to move right into constructing a preliminary outline after generating ideas this way, or you may find that you have more reading to do.

- In ***brainstorming***, you simply jot down any related ideas that come to you, in any order. Don't worry if they look unworkable or wild. Sometimes a seemingly wild idea will later generate another, more workable one.

---

*Two classic guides to such techniques are Peter Elbow, *Writing with Power: Techniques for Mastering the Writing Process* (New York: Oxford, 1981) and Gabrielle Lusser Rico, *Writing the Natural Way: Using Right-Brain Techniques to Release Your Expressive Powers* (Los Angeles: Tarcher, 1983). See also the personal accounts in more recent books by Natalie Goldberg, Sanford Kaye, and Bonnie Friedman.

- A ***cluster diagram*** is a slightly more orderly way of brainstorming. Draw a circle around the basic subject, and then start putting down other ideas that occur to you—examples, images, associations, comparisons, or whatever comes into your mind as possibly related. Draw lines to connect the subtopics to each other as well as to the central topic. You may begin to see the germ of an idea. The figure shows an example of clustering that yielded a clear research question for an urban studies course from the bare idea that something interesting was going on in the Bombay slums.

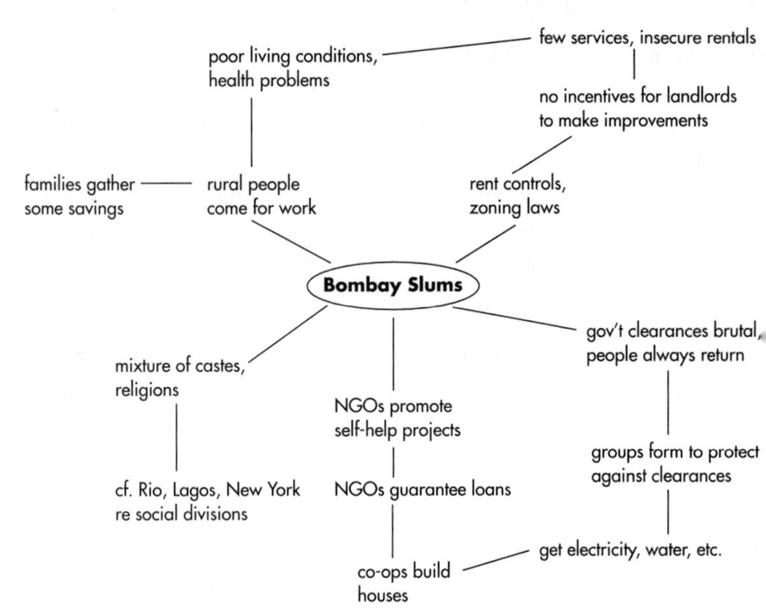

QUESTION: Relations between individuals, groups: What conditions encourage city-planning initiatives?

- ***Timed freewriting*** can help if you have lots of ideas but feel confused about where to start. Take ten or fifteen minutes and write steadily, putting down thoughts as they occur. Use sentences, but don't worry about style or structure. Just write as if you were talking to yourself.

People who suffer from **writer's block**—the inability to get text down on the page—often find that writing like this without judging the results is the best way to overcome worries that nothing they say is good enough. Sometimes it helps to turn off the screen lighting in your computer and sit there typing what comes to your mind. Keep it up for a set number of minutes without stopping.

With any freewriting, you may be surprised at how much sense your text makes. At the very least, you will uncover some questions to explore further. Perhaps you will be able to take what you wrote and create the beginnings of an outline; likely you will keep some sentences to incorporate into your paper.

3. Look for Questions to Ask

Generate questions so you can think about the problems and controversies in a topic. Remember that the biggest steps in intellectual development come not from knowing all the answers, but from asking probing questions—the tougher, the better!

- You could follow the example of journalists and ask the five W questions (and an H): *Who? What? When? Where? How?* and *Why?* For critical thinking, *How?* and *Why?* are most likely to generate ideas you can explore further, because they aim at interpreting factual information.

  Suppose in a history course you are exploring theories about the rise of neo-Naziism in present-day Germany. You might ask: *Who* are the neo-Nazis? *What* are their beliefs? *How* do they operate? *How much* support do they have? *Where* does it come from? *How* do the authorities deal with their actions? *Why* are they tolerated?

  In a psychology course, if the subject is alcoholism you might ask: *What* are the various psychological theories or perspectives about the causes of alcoholism? *How* do the different kinds of treatment reflect those theories? *How* does alcoholism in a family affect the other members? Why are children of alcoholics more likely than others to become alcoholics themselves or to marry one?

- The ***three-C approach*** outlined below makes you look at a subject from various perspectives, first breaking it up and then looking at it as a whole and in relation to other things.

  COMPONENTS

  - What are the different parts of the subject?
  - In what different ways can the subject be divided?

  CHANGE

  - What features have changed?
  - Is there a trend?
  - What caused the change?
  - What are the results of the change?

  CONTEXT

  - What other subjects is yours similar to, and how is it different from them?
  - What tradition or school of thought usually treats the subject? What other ways are there of looking at it?
  - What are the larger issues surrounding the subject?

4. Read to Enrich Your Knowledge and Opinions

To focus your analysis, you can consult both print and online resources. You may want to look at reference works, but your most intensive reading will probably focus on a few specific texts, whether scientific research papers, real-world documents, or works of literature. Chapter 2 gives detailed advice on finding what to read, doing the reading and note-taking, and integrating what you read with your own thinking. Approach all these sources with a critical perspective. Don't read just to find out *what* the authors have said; consider also *how* they have arrived at their opinions and *how* they persuade you to share them. (See page 30 on critical reading.)

Creating a Preliminary Focus Statement

Many people benefit by setting down a preliminary statement of the central point their papers will make. Here's a tactic to try, especially for big projects. Take a sentence or two and see if you can pull your thoughts together. The statement could sketch the position or thesis that you may decide to argue for, or it could state a likely solution for the problem you have been set. Often it is enough just to formulate a central question. As you begin to plan and write, your preliminary statement will give you a sense of direction. You can change the statement later as your ideas develop, but at this stage it will help you define your intentions, make your research more selective, and focus your paper. (See pages 55–56 on the qualities of a good thesis statement for a finished essay, and pages 69–70 and 79 on the introduction for reports.)

Developing Your Ideas: Some Common Patterns

Academic writing is dynamic. It doesn't just state things—it explains and demonstrates them to the reader. Here are some common ways of developing an extended flow of ideas. Note that all of these patterns are analytical: they break a subject up into parts and look at it from various angles. And they go beyond simple gathering of facts and information. They may be either **inductive** (working from facts to interpretation, as scientific reasoning does) or **deductive** (starting with a theory or concept and applying it to facts), or they may use both methods in turn. Although the reader may not notice specific organizational patterns in your finished paper, keeping one or more of them in mind can help you organize your material and show that it is logical.

1. Defining

Sometimes an entire paper is an extended definition explaining the meaning of an important, complicated, or controversial term: for example, *free trade* in economics or *postmodernism* in recent fiction. At other times a paper may begin by defining a key term and then change to another organizational pattern. Papers examining theoretical concepts often follow this pattern.

- Make a definition exact—broad enough to include everything that belongs in the category and yet narrow enough to exclude items that don't belong. A good definition acts as a kind of verbal fence around an idea, herding together all the members of the class and keeping out all outsiders. If you're defining *ordinance*, for example, distinguish it from *statute* and *regulation*.
- Also, give concrete examples and indicate how the concept works in action. These examples could vary in length from one or two sentences to several paragraphs or even pages.

2. Classifying

Classifying means grouping data into related sets. Biology, for example, traditionally classifies trees according to whether they are evergreen or deciduous, and animals as carnivores, herbivores, or omnivores. Classification may be a useful principle in any subject for making a first organization of data you have collected and will go on to interpret.

In classifying items, remember:

- Find exact titles for all sets. Check the **parallelism** among your titles as a shortcut to checking whether your sets are equivalent in type. (See pages 109–110 on parallelism.)
- If some items you want to mention are left over, add more sets or alter your existing titles to be more inclusive. Avoid having sets with only one item.
- Consider dividing sets into subsets if you want to show marked differences within sets. Use similar subtitles if possible. If you are classifying an office population according to tasks performed, for instance, you could create subsets according to sex. Then you would mark off "male" and "female" for each task.

3. Explaining a Process

This kind of organization often shows how something works—a military campaign, a social policy, or an environmental assessment.

- State the overall goal and result of the process so that you can show how the individual steps contribute to it.
- Be systematic: break down the process into steps or stages. Your order will likely be chronological, so be sure the sequence is exact and easy to follow. Start a new paragraph for each stage.

4. Tracing Causes or Effects

Cause-effect analysis is a staple of writing in all subjects. It is actually a variety of process analysis, asking and answering *why* something happened as well as *how*.

- When tracing causes, distinguish between what is a direct cause and what is merely a condition, a coincidence, or an indirect correlation. For example, if you find that more beer is consumed in the summer, and also that heart attacks rise in the summer, you can't jump to the conclusion that consumption of beer causes the heart attacks, though there may be a common cause for the two phenomena.
- Consider the most credible evidence for your subject area. In many humanities subjects, you will present elements from the book or other text you are reading. In the social sciences and sciences, your reader will expect numbers and calculations.
- In problem-solving papers, show that the solutions you propose match the causes you have named.

5. Comparing and Contrasting

Comparison is one of the most common and powerful ways to discuss a subject in depth. Use it to show that you have considered other opinions besides the one you are arguing for. Remind your reader too that your point is similar to others that are already well accepted.

- Remember that comparing means showing *differences* as well as *similarities*. Differences are often more interesting than similarities, but pointing out an unexpected similarity may be enlightening.
- Verbal analogy is considered one of the weakest forms of argument. For instance, saying that a problem is just a molehill may provide a visual image, but it doesn't help answer the reader's question about how to solve it. Don't depend on this tactic for more than an occasional special effect.
- If you use comparison as the pattern for an entire paper, your introductory and concluding paragraphs will be essential to pull together the overall point you are making about the various items.
- You can set up your comparison either item by item, or aspect by aspect. Suppose you are comparing negative and positive opinions on universal daycare. The easiest method is to discuss one set of views and then turn to the next, usually ending with the side you favour. Here is a simplified outline:

Introduction: Why New Brunswick needs to decide about universal daycare

Negative views: Costs
Feasibility
Effect on family structure
Effect on child development

Positive views: Costs
Feasibility
Effect on family structure
Effect on child development

Conclusion: The best decision on universal daycare

But this structure seems like separate papers stuck together. It works only if you bring the various views together in your introduction and conclusion and also make repeated cross-references. For this topic, you would have to repeat yourself on the negative views when you try to discuss the positive views. Choose this pattern only where the items you are comparing are so unlike that you would have to force your points into the same categories.

A more effective structure discusses the points of comparison in turn. You still need a strong introduction and conclusion to bring together your overall view, but you will likely seem more in control of the body of the paper. Here is another simplified sketch of the same topic, showing how much more central the contrasts become:

Introduction:	Why New Brunswick needs to decide about universal daycare
Costs :	Negative views Positive views
Feasibility:	Negative views Positive views
Effect on family structure:	Negative views Positive views
Effect on child development:	Negative views Positive views
Conclusion:	The best decision on universal daycare

Creating an Outline

An outline can serve as your roadmap while you draft, reminding you where you are headed and how far you have come. For a short assignment of a page or two, a few jotted lines may be enough. For a longer or more complex piece, say a ten-page essay or an intensive analytic report on an industry, a more detailed outline will help keep you on track.

An informal but well-organized point-form outline is the most frequent model. Here is an outline for an analytic essay, with notes showing the steps the writer has taken so far:

PURPOSE: To analyze the function of personal style in a political leader's work.

PRELIMINARY PERSONAL OPINION: I admire Thatcher's strength, but I suspect she lost power because people didn't really trust a woman as leader.

COURSE ISSUE, CONCEPT: How much does personality determine political events? See Celadon theory on leader fitting the times.

SOURCES: Course readings on history and theory of political leadership; UK newspaper articles (esp. editorials in *The Times*); books analyzing UK politics; Thatcher autobiography and reviews.

QUESTION: What part did Margaret Thatcher's personal style play in determining her downfall as leader?

FOCUS STATEMENT: As the Celadon theory of leadership role predicts, in the economic crises of the early 1980s, Margaret Thatcher's "strong" leadership style gained votes and built party loyalty; but in the economically stagnant 1990s the same style made her seem a block to needed actions.

I. Thatcher's early style perceived positively
    A. Charismatic ("winning horse")
        1. Public adulation—"our Maggie" at 1979 leadership conference
        2. Media awe, especially in Falklands War
        3. Reagan, Gorbachev friendships: revival of British prestige
    B. Intelligent
        1. Use of life story: scholarship girl + self-made scientist/lawyer
        2. Plain but elevated language: accent, speeches, campaign publications
        3. Comparisons to Queen
    C. Single-minded and decisive
        1. Miners' strikes
        2. Foreign alliances—compare to previous PMs
    D. Tough
        1. Labour unions
        2. Cabinet formation and party discipline
        3. Falklands War (personalized)

II. Later reversal: negative perceptions (EU negotiations, Major defection)
    A. Irritating ("schoolmarm," Boadicea)
        1. Hair, clothes, etc. (masks, schoolyard rhymes)—negative female stereotypes
        2. Media disenchantment (parodies, cartoons)
        3. Revival of Tory "wets"
    B. Out of touch
        1. Expectations of social self-reliance ("grocer's daughter")
        2. Insular outlook on foreign policy
        3. Dependence on old model of party hierarchy
    C. Confrontational
        1. Acceptance of American cruise missiles (strength of antiwar movement)
        2. Caucus scoldings—humiliation of "old boys"
        3. Bruges speech
    D. Inflexible and arrogant
        1. Treatment of universities
        2. Non-recognition of ratepayers' revolt
        3. Resistance on EU (reversal as loss)
        4. Refusal to retire

CONCLUSION: Thatcher came to power as a strong leader who could solve crises, but a decade later she lost the trust of the public, the media, and her party when she was unable to break out of the "Iron Lady" role in the face of new sets of challenges.

The principles for any outline are simple:

- ***Show your categories*** Use indentations and perhaps numbering to indicate the relationships of your points. That way you can easily see your main points as a set and also check whether you are developing each one adequately.

- ***Check lines of connection*** Be sure that each main category relates directly to the central idea (question or thesis); then see that each subcategory relates directly to the larger category that contains it.

- ***Check inner consistency*** Find the best arrangement of points and keep the sequence consistent. Discuss voters first and then political colleagues, as in the outline above, or vice versa if that is what you wish, but don't confuse the reader by mixing them randomly or suddenly dropping categories.
- ***Be prepared to change your outline during the writing process*** An outline should not confine your thinking. Since the act of writing itself will usually produce new ideas, be ready to modify your original plan if need be—then check the new plan according to the above principles.

PRACTICAL TIP

The Reverse Outline

If you feel boxed in by firm planning, or if you find you have changed your mind as you work out a draft, you can still get the benefits of outlining by using a **reverse outline**. After producing a draft, take the key idea from each paragraph or section and set it down in an indented list like the outline above. Then you can see if your ideas cover the topic adequately and are clearly related to one another.

Creating a First Draft

Drafting doesn't have to be as agonizing as many student writers think. Because of your planning and pre-thinking, your ideas are waiting to take shape on the page. All you need to do at this stage is *get something down on paper* so you can come back to edit and revise.

Approaches to Drafting

There's no one right way to produce writing. Keep in mind that the first draft is just that—only a beginning. Trust your planning! Now it's time to let your thoughts flow.

PRACTICAL TIP

Overcoming Writer's Block

You may be bothered by writer's block. Perhaps you find yourself putting off the task; or maybe you do sit down to write and just can't get your ideas down. It's a common problem, even with experienced writers. Here are some ways people have found to solve it:

- Remind yourself that a first draft can't be perfect. Save your high expectations for the revising and editing stages.
- Keep a journal of personal observations, responses, and thoughts about the topic of your paper. Don't try to organize what you write; it's just to get your thoughts flowing.
- Try out the freewriting techniques outlined on pages 5–7 in this chapter.
- Make artificial deadlines that require some minimal effort: a certain number of words each day, or an outline you can show fellow students or a counsellor at an early date. The only requirement is that something be put down on the page—with no judgements on quality.

If you're writing from an outline, you can draft your points in any order. Start where you feel confident—usually this will not be at the introduction.

After each session of drafting, jot down a few notes or questions about what you intend to say next. That will help you get back into the flow when you start again.

If you're a nervous writer, you may need to finish a whole draft before you trust yourself to start editing and revising. Or you may prefer to write and revise section by section, if you know you have trouble keeping on track. In any case, plan a reward for yourself when the draft is completed.

Using a Word Processor to Write Drafts

A word processor can help make drafting and revision easier. You ca type in material readily and then add, delete, correct, and chang passages with little fuss. Here are some suggestions for using a wor processor at the drafting stage:

- ***Type your ideas straight into the computer*** Typing speeds up th physical process for most people. Even if you're a poor typist, you' benefit by not having to recopy text. And seeing your thoughts appea *in actual words* on the screen will encourage you to keep going.
- ***Save time by using short forms in your first draft*** In the final stage you can get the word processor to insert full wordings automaticall through the "Find and Replace" function. For example, you'll sav time by typing *sa* or *ec* the first time through and then having ther changed to *sovereignty-association* or *Eschirichia coli* later. (Bu confirm each change.)
- ***Use single spacing on screen*** Don't double-space your text unt you're ready to print it out. You need to see as many lines as possib on-screen to get a sense of the flow of your work.
- ***Try different ways of organizing your paper*** Word processors let yo move blocks of text around to see how your ideas work in differer arrangements. You can combine versions easily too, since mo systems let you see a number of documents at once and copy fro one to another.
- ***Don't mistake visual quality for writing quality*** Seeing somethin typed out neatly and with a good layout may make it seem acceptabl even though the quality of the work may be poor. Don't be fooled b appearance into neglecting the editing stage. When you are close t final editing, do at least one revision from a printed copy. You will g a better sense of the whole text than when you're scrolling fro screen to screen.

- ***Save regularly and back up your files*** Nothing is more agonizing than discovering that you have lost all your work. It happens to everyone at least once—always unexpectedly. When you are writing, save every fifteen minutes or so. You can set your wordprocessing program to do this automatically; just be sure you know how to find the backup file when you need it. Then when your roommate blows the fuse, you'll lose only what you've typed since the last save. And as soon as you've finished a section of your work, copy it onto a removable disk as a spare copy. With these precautions, no breakdown will be disastrous.

A Special Situation: Collaborative Writing

Collaborative writing is common practice in the workplace, and now many instructors encourage it for course assignments. Underlying it is the notion that two heads are better than one—that collaboration is not only faster but can teach you more and produce a better product.

Warning Note: In such a collaboration, be clear about how much you are permitted to do jointly and how you should report group work. Sometimes you may need to report what each person contributed, while at other times your work will be reviewed as a team effort and graded as a whole. Some assignments call for **part-collaboration:** you plan jointly but write independently, so that the grader can give individual grades. If you are unsure about the expectations, ask your instructor.

If you are working in a **wholly collaborative writing team**, consider these tips, which others have found effective in managing the process and getting good results:

- Plan together. You should all share in analyzing the assignment, and then reach agreement about your purpose, approach, and preferred style.

- Assess individual strengths and weaknesses and assign tasks to build on strengths. Try to ensure a fairly equal distribution of work, but be flexible if someone's task becomes more demanding than expected.

- Set deadlines and create a timeline for the various activities. Put someone in charge of the time, or arrange for set meetings to ensure that the work is on schedule.
- Try to keep personal feelings separate from judgements about what works best. Be tactful when assessing other people's work, since it's easy to feel defensive or hurt when one's own writing is changed or deleted.
- Appoint one overall editor to make final editing decisions and produce a uniform style. Otherwise, especially if a number of people are creating different sections for the draft, the final version may look like a patchwork of separate pieces rather than a coherent whole.
- Double the time you first think you will need for editing. Of all the problems that can arise from group writing, rushing the editing function is the most typical and the most costly. See the next section for essential advice.

Editing

Editing means looking at the piece as a whole to preview it for the eventual reader. It involves seeing whether the ideas are (1) well organized, (2) well supported, and (3) well expressed. It usually leads to rewriting, and more satisfaction afterwards when you see that you've said what you wanted to say. It's much more than proofreading, though it involves some checking of details. Good editing can transform a mediocre first draft into an excellent final version.

Start Large, End Small

Editing may mean adding paragraphs, deleting others, shifting others around, and reshaping still others. It usually means adding, deleting, shifting, and reshaping sentences and phrases. Look at the big picture before tackling sentence structure, diction, style, and documentation.

1. Look first at overall *organization*. If you are using a word processor, print out everything so that you can view the entire document. Then consider these questions:
   - Is each section in the right place to fulfill your purpose? (It might help to make a list or reverse outline, section by section. See pages 13–16.)
   - Is each section connected to what came before and what follows? (Look for logical meaning as well as transitional words and phrases.)
   - If a reader were to begin with your introductory section, would he or she know where you are headed? (Ask an obliging roommate or other friend to give you an opinion.)
   - Would a person reading your conclusion know what question you had asked and how you had arrived at your answer? (Again, try this out on somebody else. Don't settle for a polite *yes*—see if the reader can give an actual paraphrase.)
2. Then check whether you have set out the *reasoning* you intended. Look back at the assignment sheet, and be sure you can answer yes to these questions:
   - Have you performed the kind of thinking the assignment sheet asked for (for example, *analyze, argue, compare, explore*)? (See page 3 for a discussion of these verbs.)
   - Have you used concepts and methods of reasoning discussed in the course? Beware especially of just retelling stories and listing information. (See pages 9–13 on common patterns for developing ideas analytically.)
   - Have you stated your overall point clearly? Do you use topic sentences to guide your reader through the stages of your reasoning? (See page 103 on the uses of topic sentences.)
   - Have you given adequate evidence for your argument or interpretation? (A quick way of checking is to examine your

paragraph development. See pages 103–106 on ways of developing paragraphs.)

3. Now *polish your style* by moving to smaller matters such as word choice, sentence structure, grammar, punctuation, and spelling. You may already have marked passages that you know need further work. (See Chapters 7 to 9 for guidance, especially the checklists reminding you what to look for.)

- Use the spell checker that comes with your wordprocessing program. It will help you catch most typos and many wrongly spelled words. But don't let it replace anything automatically, or you'll end up with nonsense words. It can't tell you the right spelling for names or technical words. It also won't tell you when you have used a word wrongly (such as *their* for *there*) or when you've typed the wrong word (*form* when you meant *from*, or *not* instead of *now*, for instance). So you will still have to read through your piece and use a print dictionary to look up words that you suspect are not right.

- Don't depend on a grammar checker. The best ones still miss many errors, and they give bad advice frequently. If you know that you overuse slang or the passive voice, you may find some of the "hits" useful, but be sure to make your own choice of replacement phrases. You may gain some knowledge too if you take the time to read the explanation screens. But nothing can substitute for your own considered judgement.

Find Some Preliminary Readers

You may be able to show your draft to your instructor, a tutor, or even fellow students. Check whether this practice is allowed or encouraged at your school. Here are some tips for making the most of such opportunities—and also for staying within the bounds of legality.

- Consider the session a chance for oral discussion, not for making actual changes in the paper. You are the one responsible for everything that ends up on the page. Leave plenty of time to do further individual work after the session.

- Know what you have accomplished so far, and be able to say what you would like to work on. Don't ask "Do you like it?" or "What's wrong with it?", but "What is the main point you see in that paragraph?" and "What needs clarifying?"

- Beware of following suggestions without understanding them. Untrained people can create more errors than they correct. Ask for explanations and check with a dictionary or handbook.

Consider the Appearance

Looks do count. Give your instructor the pleasure of reading a neat and clear presentation. These are the basic expectations for any type of assignment. (See also pages 82–87 for specific advice on format for reports, and pages 95–96 on format for résumés.)

- ***Include a cover page*** giving the title of your paper, the name of the course, your name, the date, and the instructor's name. Don't bother with coloured paper, fancy print, or decorative illustrations.

- ***Double-space*** your text, including indented quotations, footnotes, and reference lists.

- ***Leave margins*** of one inch (2.5 cm) on all sides of the page.

- ***Use a standard font in twelve-point size.***

- ***Leave your right-hand margins unjustified*** for easier reading.

- ***Number your pages*** in the top right-hand corner. Omit the number for the first page of your paper (since it will be headed by the title), starting in with the number *2* on the second page.

- ***Put the reference list or bibliography*** on a separate page at the end. (See pages 35–53 for different documentation formats.)

- ***Staple*** your pages rather than using a bulky binding.

CHAP

SOURCES: Building on Other Texts

When you produce academic assignments, you don't just write alone—you build on what other people have written. You bring together material with different viewpoints, and sometimes you reject or rethink what you read.

This chapter is about ways to select and read typical kinds of material, outlining the skills you need and the choices you face at different stages. Because electronic indexing and publication methods make retrieving information simple, we concentrate especially on choosing from the wealth of resources available and making what you read part of your own thinking.

Choosing Research Sources

The amount of information available on any topic can be overwhelming. Whether you start from an open topic or a closely prescribed one, you will need to be selective.

Seeing the Big Picture

To avoid a "dead-end" path, do some **overview reading** first, perhaps while you're still defining your exact approach to the topic. This reading can start you thinking about where you're going, though it can't provide the whole basis for a thoughtful piece of writing. Start by reviewing your course outline, class notes, and textbook to see what you're expected to know in terms of the course. Then look at encyclopedias and other reference works.

This reading is your chance to brush up on **common knowledge** in your field. The term doesn't refer to things everybody knows, but to ideas that are generally accepted by people who take an interest in the topic. You don't have to explain these things at length in your paper unless you're asked to. But you need to know for yourself what they are, and to use the terms correctly. Much of common knowledge is simply factual: that the First World War ended in 1918, for instance, or that Montana borders on Canada. These are undisputed ideas, even if people don't always know them without looking them up. Standard concepts in a field may also qualify as common knowledge: *titration* for a chemistry report, or *blank verse* for literary studies, for instance.

The reading will also give you a sense of who the **experts** in the field are and what **issues** they're exploring. Look especially for disagreements and gaps in what's being said. Be ready to make connections too with other readings in the course and topics you're exploring in other courses.

General encyclopedias, including those in CD-ROM form, can give an overview of historical events, figures, or movements. Even more useful are **specialized encyclopedias** (also sometimes available in CD-ROM) containing short articles by experts, summarizing facts and thinking in specific areas of study. Though never quite up to date, they're full of useful and stimulating material. Your instructor or a librarian will guide you if you're wondering which works of this kind would be suitable for your project. Here are a few samples, suggesting the range of material available:

- ***The Cambridge Guide to World Theatre***. Ed. Martin Banham. Cambridge: Cambridge UP, 1988.
- ***The Canadian Encyclopedia***, 2nd ed. 4 vols. Ed. Bruce M. March. Edmonton: Hurtig, 1988.
- ***The Encyclopedia of Religion***. 16 vols. Ed. Mircea Eliade. New York: Macmillan, 1987.
- ***Grzimek's Encyclopedia of Mammals***. 5 vols. Ed. Bernhard Grzimek. New York: McGraw- Hill, 1990.
- ***The McGraw-Hill Encyclopedia of Science and Technology***, 7th ed. 20 vols. New York: McGraw-Hill, 1992.
- ***The New Grove Dictionary of Music and Musicians***. 20 vols. Ed. Stanley Sadie. London: Macmillan, 1980.

The **World Wide Web** can also function like a big, disorganized encyclopedia if you want stimulating glimpses of new scientific knowledge or lively thoughts on contemporary issues. Use a **search engine**—a method of finding Web pages that contain specific words or phrases—to get some starts in your subject area, or begin from a university home page. Then follow links to get as close as possible to your topic. But remember that material on the Web isn't always trustworthy or fair. Much of it doesn't meet the criteria set out below for judging worthwhile sources (pages 28–29).

Recognizing Different Kinds of Research Material

Once you have a sense of what questions interest you and what material is available to explore them, you need to find specific readings to focus and extend your thinking. You will read these different kinds of sources in different ways:

Primary material gives you direct contact with an event or person. Examples are copies of historical treaties, letters or diaries, and data gathered in experiments or field work. Works of literature and philosophy also belong in this category because you can experience them directly.

Read primary documents **intensively**, taking notes as you go. You may well want to quote and analyze specific words or phrases in your paper.

Secondary material consists of what others have said about a topic. Examples are biographies, interpretations of literary or philosophical works, discussions of scientific data, and studies of issues. Reading secondary material can be stimulating, but reading too much may submerge your own thinking.

Read secondary material **selectively**. Take notes about key arguments so you remember who wrote what and begin to see how the various views relate.

Using Search Terms

To find material that exactly fits your topic and approach, you will likely do some searching by subject category. That can be effective if you know how to name your topic in terms that fit the database system or index. Here are some general pointers; ask a librarian for guidance through specific systems and types of indexes.

To come up with **key terms**, start with the most specific noun that fits your topic. A technical term like *Locusta* will get you right to the material you need for a zoology paper, whereas *locust* will get too much, some of it not on your topic at all. Also try synonyms in turn: *wedding* and then *marriage* and then *matrimony* or *nuptials*. Finding good second and third terms can focus your search even further: not just *Civil War, US,* but also *nursing*.

You can also use partial or **truncated words** to get all the items with different endings on the root term: for instance, *welding* and *welded* as well as *weld*. Find out what symbol to type after the root form of the word, in this case *weld*.

Boolean searching uses commands that indicate the relationship of the various search terms. Ordinarily, if you type in two terms you get a list of items that include both, as if you had put *AND* between them. Some databases let you type in *OR* instead, giving you items with either one of the terms. And some can use *NOT*, letting you weed out anticipated mismatches: *rock NOT music* will get what you need for geology, for instance.

Judging Material

From the huge store of potential sources, which are most suitable? Here are some fast criteria for making an initial (not final) judgement about a printed source; they may also help you assess the worth of online material:

- It is in a university or college library, or a Web site sponsored by an academic or professional organization. Librarians, faculty, and professional officers have likely selected trustworthy material.
- It was published recently, preferably within the last five years. If you want to use an older, "classic" work, also choose versions that were published lately.
- It was published by a reputable publisher, often a university press. That means that it has been **peer-reviewed**—evaluated and checked by experts in the field.
- It identifies its own sources in notes and a reference list, or links in a Web file, implying that the author is willing to have readers check its accuracy and fairness.

The Special Qualities of Journal Articles

If you're asked to use **journal articles**, don't confuse them with magazine pieces. Journals are academic periodicals where experts publish their research—they contain the latest news in specialized fields. Their articles are peer-reviewed (checked by other experts), and they always acknowledge their sources in notes and reference lists. They often include abstracts at the beginning of each piece. The only ads are for other books or journals. One look at the pages of solid text in an academic journal will tell you that it isn't meant for popular entertainment! It's true that some magazines such as *Harper's, The Economist,* and *New Scientist* may provide useful overviews of current research or hot issues, but they aren't considered as trustworthy or thorough as academic journals. Read them only for stimulus and follow up their references to other sources—including the journal articles on which they were probably based.

Quick **skimming** can also help you decide about material. Look over the tables of contents, prefaces, and introductions. Watch for ideas you recognize, and notice new combinations or angles. In the case of journal articles, read through the abstract or the first paragraph to confirm whether the item covers the right topic, and whether the level of technicality is within your grasp. For guidance about books, you can take a quick look at what other experts have said about them. *The Book Review Digest* (probably available in your library's reference room) summarizes reviews published within a couple of years of the book's publication.

Reading Your Sources

Read actively—don't try to become a sponge. Here are some steps for effective reading, showing how to integrate your reading with your overall goals for the paper.

PRACTICAL TIP

Critical Reading

You will probably hear that you should *read critically*, as well as think critically and write critically. That doesn't mean reading with a negative attitude, ready to complain. It does mean reading with awareness and care. Here are some aspects:

- **Be aware of the author's intentions.** Look especially for the author's thesis (or hypothesis) and conclusion, and for the topic sentences that mark stages in the presentation.
- **Distinguish between fact and opinion.** You want both, but should notice how interpretations are offered. When you find a useful point, note whether it comes from data gathered by observation or is built on speculation.
- **Look for assumptions and omissions.** Note the ways the author connects ideas. Is it taken for granted that one thing causes another, or that something is more important than something else? Similarly, if factors are neglected, ask why.
- **Make comparisons with other material on the subject.** As you read each piece, remind yourself what other views are possible. Be pleased, in fact, when you find disagreements—you've found something to write about.
- **Know what your own reactions are.** Your puzzlements and objections and new insights will be part of your own discussion of the subject.

1. ***Seek*** Jot down questions for which you want answers—perhaps factual matters, but also definitions you need clarified, issues for interpretation, connections you're wondering about.
2. ***Survey*** Before starting to read any piece, get an idea of its structure by looking at the title, the section headings, and the first sentences of

a few paragraphs. Skim the abstract or introduction to see what the main point is, and then the conclusion to see where the discussion went.

. *Find* As you read through each piece, relate the material to your earlier questions. Note what reasoning is provided, and whether the answers are convincing.

aking Useful Notes

Writing things down can help you read more attentively and urposively. Try to record only what will be useful when you are writing our own paper.

Here are some tips:

Make a master list Write up a bibliography entry for each item as soon as you get hold of it, using the documentation format you need for your paper (see pages 35–53). Take a coloured page or coloured cards that you can find again easily, or use a separate computer file that will give you a premade bibliography when you need it.

Don't write down too much Mostly summarize rather than copy, since you shouldn't rely on long quotations in your paper. A common misjudgement is to highlight or underline vast amounts. It's better to keep a pencil at hand for making marginal notes—a few only, and in your own words.

Use portable notes For convenience, try writing your notes on "stickies." Then detach them later and arrange them on a card or piece of paper. That method is especially useful for library books. Write down a page number for each note.

Label your notes Label each of your notecards (or sections in your notebook) according to its topic. Eventually you will be able to lay out the set of notes and try different groupings—and you may see an outline start to take shape.

Acknowledging Sources

Academic knowledge is largely stored in books and journals. To establis that you share some of that knowledge, your papers need to say wha you've read. That's the real reason for going to the trouble o acknowledging your sources—not just to avoid accusations of plagiarism

The terms *acknowledgement, citation, referencing,* and *documenta tion* all refer to the same practice: letting your readers know what yo have read and how your ideas are related to those of your sources. You instructors may call it by any of those names.

When to Cite Sources

Knowing when you have "borrowed" an idea isn't always easy. Her are some common questions students ask, and basic answers for them

- **I didn't know anything about the subject until I started this paper So do I have to give a reference for every point I make?** You'r safer to over-reference than to skimp. But you can cut down th clutter by recognizing that some ideas are common knowledge i the field (see page 25), that is, accepted by people knowledgeabl about the topic. Check with your instructor if you're in doubt whethe a specific point is considered common knowledge in your field.
- **Can't I avoid problems just by listing every source in th bibliography?** No, you need to integrate your acknowledgement with what you're saying. That may mean repeating "X says" and " argues against X." And remember that you must identify paraphrase or summaries even if they're not in quotation marks.
- **If I put the ideas into my own words, do I still have to clog up m pages with all those names and numbers?** Sorry—yes, you do. Yo can use your own words because that saves space and lets yo connect ideas smoothly. But whether you quote a passage directly i quotation marks, paraphrase it closely in your own words, or jus summarize it rapidly, you need to identify the source.

- **How can I tell what's my own idea and what has come from somebody else?** Careful note-taking helps, so you know what names and dates to attach to ideas. Try making a deliberate effort, as you go through your readings, to work out connections among ideas. Look for contrasts as well as similarities, and note questions or objections of your own. If you find that most of the references in your draft come from a few books or articles, look for other sources that take a different tack—then write about the differences.

- **What kinds of ideas do I have to acknowledge?** With experience reading academic prose, you'll soon get used to the way writers in your field refer to their sources. Here are the main times you should give acknowledgements:

To refer to a specific passage. In literary studies you'll quote often (mostly in small amounts), but in most other disciplines you'll quote only when the original words are especially memorable. Note the way that mentioning the author's name helps indicate where the borrowing starts and stops.

> Northrop Frye discusses comedy in terms of the spring spirit, the infusion of new life and hope into human awareness of universal problems.[7] The ending of *The Tempest* exemplifies this pattern. *[traditional endnote or footnote format for humanities]*

To give particular facts as evidence. When you're relying on facts that are little-known or might be disputed by people in your discipline, establish that they're trustworthy by referring to authoritative sources—thus paying tribute to others makes your own viewpoint more credible.

> In September 1914, more than 1300 skirmishes were recorded on the Western Front (Taylor 337). *[MLA format for humanities]*

> Other recent researchers (4,11,12), in their discussion of pancreatic pseudocysts, confirm my finding that drug treatment has little effect. *[Vancouver format for biomedical sciences]*

To refer to others' ideas or opinions, whether you agree with them or not. The way you phrase your acknowledgement can indicate your attitude to the source and lead into your own argument.

> One writer (Von Daniken, 1970) even asserts that the Great Pyramid was built for the practical purpose of guiding navigation. *[APA format for social sciences]*

Integrating Sources with Your Own Writing

People who read student papers often complain of a "patchwork quilt" effect. They feel they're seeing pieces cut out of sources and stitched together to cover the topic. Here are some ways to show that you have woven your reading into the fabric of your thinking:

- ***Let your own words dominate*** at all times. Summarize rather than paraphrasing closely; quote only for special effect. Create your own wording especially for topic sentences and thesis statements.
- ***Comment*** on the borrowed ideas, especially when you're giving an extended summary. Try sometimes to put borrowed ideas in subordinate clauses ("Although Tyyska has established" or "When Khan asserts") so that your sentences move immediately to your own comment or counterargument.
- ***Mention authors' names*** in your sentences to show you know where specific ideas come from and indicate that the other ideas are yours. (But don't do this for an assignment in the sciences. Science writing rarely mentions researchers by name except in the reference list.)
- ***Choose your verbs*** to show your attitude toward each source you mention. Note the different effects in these samples, and note how some lead attention back toward your development of the idea:

As Smith **says**, stone is hard.	[Smith confirms what we already thought.]

Smith **shows** that stone is hard.	[His evidence is trustworthy.]
Smith **suggests** that stone is hard.	[He treats his evidence fairly.]
Smith **claims** that stone is hard.	[He doesn't make a good case for it.]

- ***Look for disagreements*** among your sources and comment on them. You may be able to point out, for example, how the sources rely on different evidence or interpret the same evidence in different ways.

Standard Formats for Documenting Sources

The systems for giving references are meant to let the reader easily see how good your sources are (that is, how up to date, authoritative, and wide-ranging.) Different disciplines have their own expected formats, each with its own logic. You can master its main aspects and learn how to look up the details.

Here's a trade secret that may lighten the burden: most instructors care much more about how well you understand and use your sources than about the way you format your references. Even if you don't get all the details perfect, you'll probably be forgiven if you show the basic information—author, title of work, and date.

Here are examples and guidelines for the four most common systems. Concentrate on learning one system fairly thoroughly; then you will know what elements to look out for when you have to use another one.

1. MLA System (Parenthetical Author-Page References)

This streamlined format, developed by the Modern Language Association (MLA), is now the one most **humanities** instructors expect. Every time you refer to a source in your paper, you put parentheses inside your sentence to name the author and give the page number. *The MLA Handbook for Writers of Research Papers* by Joseph Gibaldi and Walter Achtert gives detailed guidance and examples.

> When Hamlet protests to Gertrude, "Leave wringing of your hands" (2) (3.4.35), he is naming a common gesture of Elizabethan actors. Physical movements of this sort, as Ambrese says in her *Renaissance Stage*, were a standard technique for projecting emotion (3) (34). Shakespeare's audiences, in fact, would have recognized hand-wringing as a specific signal meaning "ague of the spirits" (Reynolds (4) qtd. in Mahieu (1) 431), and might have seen that it was similar to gestures used in the old tradition of religious plays (5) (Termagant Society). Hamlet has this tradition in mind when he warns the players at Elsinore not to debase their play by "out-herod[ing] Herod":
>
> > Nor do not saw the air too much with your hand, thus, but use all gently....O, it offends me to the soul to hear a robustious periwig-pated fellow tear a passion to tatters, to very rags, to split the ears of the groundlings, who, for the most part, are capable of nothing but inexplicable dumb shows and noise. (3.2.4-12) (6)

Here are guidelines for handling some key details of the MLA system, as shown in the example opposite:

1. Use parentheses within your sentences to identify sources. Give author and page number for identification.

2. To identify a quotation from a primary source that is the main topic of your paper, give only the page or other identifying numbers. Here, the numbers refer to act, scene, and line from a play. The author, Shakespeare, is already evident from context.

3. To refer to a secondary source, give author and page (but not date). Here, the author's name, Ambrese, has already been used in the sentence.

4. Use the abbreviation "qtd." to cite a quotation you have seen in another author's work. In the reference list, name only the source where you saw the quotation. Here, you read Mahieu, not Reynolds.

5. Since a Web file is not divided into pages, give only the name of the author. Here, the author is a group.

6. Indent a quotation of four or more lines, and don't use quotation marks. Put the citation for an indented quotation at the right margin.

Basic Formula for MLA System

PRACTICAL TIP

IN YOUR PAPER (Lastname page)

IN "WORKS CONSULTED" LIST:

Book Lastname, Firstname. *Title of Book: Subtitle of Book.* City: Publisher, year.

Article Lastname, Firstname. "Title of Article: Subtitle of Article." *Journal Title*, volume (year): firstpage-lastpage.

7

Works Consulted

8

Ambrese, Jean. *The Renaissance Stage*. New York: Oxford UP, 1997.

9 10

—-. "Renovating *Hamlet* for Contemporary Audiences." *UTQ*, 53 (1994): 431-42.

Mahieu, Aline. *Acting Shakespeare*. New York: Gibson, 1995.

11

Shakespeare, William. *Hamlet. The Norton Introduction to Literature*. 4th ed. Ed. Carl E. Bain, Jerome Beaty, and J. Paul Hunter. New York: Norton, 1986. 273-98.

12

Stoppard, Tom. *Rosencrantz and Guildenstern Are Dead*. Perf. William Mills and Evan Cameron. Dir. Alison Sills. Videocassette. YBO, 1998.

13

Tawney, Linda. "New Focus for Research: Hands in Morality Plays." Online posting. Newsgroup comp.edu.drama.renaissance. 7 Feb. 1998.

14

Termagant Society. "Morality-Play Acting Methods." http://www.winston.edu/socs/termag/acting.html. July 1997.

(7) Name your reference list "Works Consulted" if it includes all items you read, even if you didn't refer to all of them in your text. Name it "Works Cited" if you referred in your text to all the items.

(8) List the items by authors' last names in alphabetical order, with first lines at the left margin and subsequent lines indented. Italicize titles of books and journals (or underline them if your printer does not print italics), but use quotation marks around titles of articles and poems. Use the briefest possible form of the publisher's name. Put periods between the sections of each entry.

(9) To cite a second piece by the same author, use three hyphens instead of retyping the name. (If you had referred to both pieces in the text, you would have included short-form titles in your parentheses to distinguish between them [for example, Ambrese, *Stage* 434 and Ambrese, "Renovating" 442].)

(10) Use initials for the titles of well-known journals. Give volume number and, as confirmation, the year in parentheses. (For a magazine or newspaper article you would give the full date of publication and then the page number.)

(11) List a source that is part of a collection under that source's author and title; then give information about the collection, including editors. Indicate the source's page numbers in the collection.

(12) For a performance or other non-print source, give enough information about creators, performers, location, and so on, to let your readers know which version you have used.

(13) For any electronic document, name the medium and give enough other information for readers to find the item themselves. Here, a newsgroup posting is cited, so the name of the newsgroup and the date of the posting may be helpful.

(14) For a Web file, give the full URL (online address).

2. Endnotes/Footnotes System (Traditional)

Some humanities professors and **a few science disciplines** will ask you to use the traditional system of small raised numbers referring to footnotes or endnotes, followed by a bibliography. They prefer this system because it causes little interruption of your prose. A section at the back of the *MLA Handbook for Writers of Research Papers* by Joseph Gibaldi and Walter Achtert outlines the main elements.

Here is an example of the same humanities essay as above, this time using endnotes:

> When Hamlet protests to Gertrude, "Leave wringing of your hands,"[1] he is naming a common gesture of Elizabethan actors. Physical movements of this sort, Ambrese says in her *Renaissance Stage*, were a standard technique for projecting emotion.[2] Shakespeare's audiences, in fact, would have recognized hand-wringing as a specific signal meaning "ague of the spirits,"[3] and might have felt its similarity to gestures used in the old tradition of religious plays.[4] Hamlet has this tradition in mind when he warns the players at Elsinore not to debase their play by "out-herod[ing] Herod":
>
> > Nor do not saw the air too much with your hand, thus, but use all gently.... O, it offends me to the soul to hear a robustious periwig-pated fellow tear a passion to tatters, to very rags, to split the ears of the groundlings, who, for the most part, are capable of nothing but inexplicable dumb shows and noise. (III.ii.4-12)

Here are guidelines for handling some key details of the traditional endnote or footnote system, as shown in the example opposite:

1. Use the footnote or endnote function in your word processor to create this system of small raised numbers or **superscripts** and notes to match them. (Either footnotes or endnotes are acceptable to most professors.) Put the note numbers after other sentence punctuation.

2. For the first reference to a primary source, use a note to let the reader know which edition you are using. For further references to this source, you can just give the page or other identifying numbers. Here, the numbers refer to act, scene, and line from a play. They could be either Roman numerals, as here, or ordinary Arabic numerals (3.2.4-12.).

3. Indent a quotation of more than four or five lines, and don't use quotation marks. Then put the citation over at the right margin.

Footnotes or Endnotes in Any System

Even when you're using one of the parenthetical systems, you may use footnotes or endnotes to give "asides"—ideas that don't quite fit the structure of your paragraph but are worth introducing for interest's sake.

Notes

(4)

[1] William Shakespeare, *Hamlet*, in *The Norton Introduction to Literature*, 4th ed., ed. Carl E. Bain, Jerome Beaty, and J. Paul Hunter (New York: Norton, 1986), III.iv.35. All subsequent references will be to this edition.

[2] Jean Ambrese, *The Renaissance Stage* (New York: Oxford UP, 1997), 34.

[3] For instance, a handbook of acting published in 1587 listed seventeen standard motions of the hand. Peter Reynolds, *The Player's Chapbooke*, (5) qtd. in Aline Mahieu, *Acting Shakespeare* (New York: Gibson, 1995), 431.

[4] Termagant Society, "Morality-Play Acting Methods" (http://www.winston.edu/socs/termag/acting.html, July 1997).

(6) Bibliography

(7)

Ambrese, Jean. *The Renaissance Stage*. New York: Oxford UP, 1997.

(8)

—. "Renovating Hamlet for Contemporary Audiences." *UTQ*, 53 (1994): 431-42.

Mahieu, Aline. *Acting Shakespeare*. New York: Gibson, 1995.

(4) In the Notes, indent and number the first line of each note. Give the author's given name and then family name, with commas between sections of the entry, and put parentheses around publication data. End with the page number if any.

(5) In the Bibliography, use the abbreviation "qtd." to cite a quotation you have seen in another author's work. List only the source where you saw the quotation. Here, you read Mahieu, not Reynolds.

(6) Use the title "Bibliography" for a list of all the works you have read, even if you didn't quote them all in the paper.

(7) Follow the same format for entries as in the MLA system. List the items by authors' last names in alphabetical order, with first lines at the left margin and subsequent lines indented. Italicize titles of books and journals (or underline them if your printer does not print italics), but use quotation marks around titles of articles and poems. Use the briefest possible form of the publisher's name. Put periods between the sections of each entry.

(8) To cite a second piece by the same author, use three hyphens instead of retyping the name.

(9)

Shakespeare, William. *Hamlet. The Norton Introduction to Literature.* 4th ed. Ed. Carl E. Bain, Jerome Beaty, and J. Paul Hunter. New York: Norton, 1986. 273-98.

(10)

Stoppard, Tom. *Rosencrantz and Guildenstern Are Dead*. Perf. William Mills and Evan Cameron. Dir. Alison Sills. Videocassette. YBO, 1998.

(11)

Tawney, Linda. "New Focus for Research: Hands in Morality Plays." Online posting. Newsgroup comp.edu.drama.renaissance. 7 Feb. 1998.

(12)

Termagant Society. "Morality-Play Acting Methods." http://www.winston.edu/socs/termag/acting.html. July 1997.

(9) List a source that is part of a collection under that source's author and title; then give information about the collection, including editors. Indicate the page numbers within the collection.

(10) For a performance or other non-print source, give enough information about creators, performers, location, and so on, to let your readers know which version you have used.

(11) For an electronic document, name the medium and give enough other information for readers to find the item themselves. Here, a newsgroup posting is cited, so the name of the newsgroup and the date of the posting may be helpful.

(12) For a Web file, give the full URL (online address).

Basic Formula for Endnotes/ Footnotes System

PRACTICAL TIP

IN YOUR PAPER

Book [superscript number]

Article [superscript number]

IN YOUR NOTES

Book [number] Firstname Lastname, *Title of Book: Subtitle of Book* (City: Publisher, year) pages.

Article [number] Firstname Lastname, "Title of Article: Subtitle of Article," *Journal Title*, volume (year): pages.

IN YOUR BIBLIOGRAPHY

Book Lastname, Firstname. *Title of Book: Subtitle of Book.* City: Publisher, year.

Article Lastname, Firstname. "Title of Article: Subtitle of Article." *Journal Title*, volume (year): firstpage-lastpage.

3. APA System (Parenthetical Author-Date References)

The **social sciences, management studies,** and **many of the sciences** emphasize authors and publication dates for sources. Every time you refer to a source, you put parentheses inside your sentence to name the author and give the year of publication. The American Psychological Association (APA) has developed the most commonly used system; see the *Publication Manual* for a detailed explanation. Here's an example in strict APA format, including the use of old-fashioned underlining instead of italics. Ask if your instructor prefers a variation, and look at journals in your own discipline for models:

> ①
>
> Pinker (1994) argues that humans use language in complex forms because they are biologically constructed to communicate information, not because they are taught to communicate. He calls language "one of
>
> ② ③
>
> nature's engineering marvels" (p. 19), and quotes Darwin's idea that the ability to learn language is "an instinctive tendency to acquire an art"
>
> ③
>
> (p. 20). The language acquisition of deaf children provides a good way to test his thesis. Pinker cites the study by Quentin and Feng (1993) on the highly developed use of American Sign Language among profoundly deaf children who learn it before the age of six. The data now being gathered about creolised sign language among Nicaraguan children
>
> ④
>
> (Rama, 1996; Singh, 1997) further support his argument. However, preliminary accounts of Millie, a deaf "wild child" currently being

Here are guidelines for handling some key details of the APA system, as shown in the example opposite:

1. Use parentheses within your sentences for all citations. Give the author and year of publication for every citation. Here, the author's name is already part of your sentence.

2. Give the page number for each quotation. Giving it for a paraphrase or summary is optional.

3. When you cite an author you have seen quoted in another author's work, give the reference to the source where you saw the quotation. (Here, you read Pinker, not Darwin.)

4. You can cite more than one source at a time within a single set of parentheses. Separate the items by semicolons.

PRACTICAL TIP

Basic Formula for APA System

IN YOUR PAPER

Book	(Lastname, year)
Article	(Lastname, year)

IN YOUR WORKS CITED OR REFERENCES LIST

Book	Lastname, Initial. (year). *Title of book: Subtitle of book.* City: Publisher.
Article	Lastname, Initial. (year). Title of article: Subtitle of article. *Journal Title, volume*, firstpage-lastpage.

studied in Australia (e.g., Urmilla, 1997; Zarenko, 1998), suggest that Pinker's thesis does not pay enough attention to environmental differences.

(5) Works Cited

(6) Pinker, S. (1994). *The language instinct: How the mind creates language*. New York: Morrow.

Quentin, R. J. & Feng, F. Z. (1993). The critical period and ASL: Evidence of a readiness window. *New Zealand Journal of Speech Therapy*, 14, 1104-1123.

(7) Rama, P. J. (1994). Spontaneous development of a creole language. In B. Mills & M. Cameron (Eds.), *Teaching the deaf* (pp. 517-632). Englewood Cliffs, NJ: Prentice Hall.

Singh, J. (1996). Introduction to T. N. Aferian, *Mind and matter: Ideas from the field* (pp. i- xii). Toronto: Allyn & Bacon.

Urmilla, J. (1998, January 15). Millie's development. *New York Times*, pp. (8) A2, A6.

Zarenko, P. (1998). "Wild" children now: Millie. Web site (9) http://www.evans.edu/~zarenko/wild/millie.html.

(5) Name your reference list "Works Cited" to list only works you have actually referred to in your paper. If you include other works you have read that are relevant to your topic, you could call that list "References" or "Bibliography."

(6) List the items by the first author's last name in alphabetical order, with the first line indented. Use only initials for authors' given names. Put the year of publication in parentheses as the second item in each entry. For titles and subtitles of books and journals, capitalize only the first word; but capitalize journal titles as in the original. Do not use quotation marks around article titles. Underline titles of books and journals (or italicize them if you are not following the strict format rules), including volume numbers and subsequent punctuation. Use brief forms of publishers' names. Put periods between the sections of each entry.

(7) List a source that is part of a collection under its own author and title; then give information about the collection, including editors. Indicate page numbers within the collection.

(8) Give the exact date of publication for a newspaper or magazine piece, and identify the section as well as the page number.

(9) For an electronic document, name the medium and give enough other information for readers to find the item and read it for themselves. For a Web file, give the full URL, online address. Increasingly, writers specify "available" before the URL or e-mail address.

4. Numbered-List Systems (for example, Vancouver Format)

The **sciences** use many different documentation formats, including adaptations of those used by the humanities and social sciences. Some science disciplines use numbered notes in the text, referring to a numbered list of sources at the end of the paper—a simple way to cut down clutter in your prose. The very compressed format shown here, widely accepted in the **biomedical sciences**, was worked out by editors at a meeting in Vancouver. If you have to master the details of such a system, look at the entries in a scholarly journal that uses it or consult a guidebook such as Edward J. Huth, *Medical Style and Format: An International Manual for Authors, Editors, and Publishers.* Specialized referencing software can help format the tricky punctuation.

Gastrointestinal symptoms have been found to be related to specific ① life crises (1,2) such as marriage, retirement, or bereavement. Nausea in particular often lacks an organic cause, but can be correlated with ② stressful events (1,3). It is more frequent among females than males (2,4) and most debilitating for women over 80 years of age ③ (5). Some evidence exists that a tendency to nausea is inherited (6,7).

④ References

⑤

1. You CH, Lee KY, Chey RY, Menguy R. Electrogastrographic study of patients with unexplained nausea, bloating and vomiting. Gastroenterology 1990;89:311-4.

Here are guidelines for handling some key details of the numbered-list system, as shown in the example opposite in the Vancouver format:

1. To refer to a source, use ordinary-size numbers inside parentheses in your sentence. The numbers refer to entries in the references list.

2. You may refer to sources more than once, using the same numbers as on the first reference.

3. Whenever possible, put citations at the ends of sentences, and do not quote from sources or mention authors' names within your sentences, except where you want to comment extensively.

4. Call the reference list simply "References." List only sources you have actually cited in your paper.

5. List the entries in the order in which you have mentioned them in your paper. Put the reference numbers at the left-hand margin and then indent the text of each entry. Use initials for authors' given names, with no comma before or periods after them. Use no italics or quotation marks. Put periods (as shown) between the main sections of the entries. Use the shortest possible form for second numbers in page ranges.

2. Dauphin J, Colomba J. Nausea as symptom in school-entering children. In: Sodeman WA, ed. Stress-related illness. Copenhagen: Munksgaard, 1993:12-8.
3. Seaman WB. The case of the pancreatic pseudocyst. Hosp Pract 1981;16(Sep):24-5.
4. Munk M. Presenting symptoms of anorexia. Emerg Med 1997;25(Oct):39-46.
5. Brama T. Effects of continuing nausea on very elderly females. Geront 1996;36(Jun): 1146-53.
6. Phoney RG. Heredity: a medical guide. 5th ed. Oxford: Blackwell, 1997: 310-9.
7. Wu N. Focal index: a new parameter to evaluate hereditary risks of gastric ailments. Stomach Institute Web site 1997 (Sep). http://www.stomach/statsnews/focal.html.

6. List an article or chapter in a collection under the author's name. Then give the editor's name, the title, and full publication information for the collection.

7. For journal articles, use the accepted abbreviations for the journal titles, followed by year, volume number, and page numbers. Use a semicolon between date and volume number and a colon before the page numbers, with no spaces after them.

8. For articles in journals, insert an abbreviation of the month after the issue number.

9. In references to books, give the range of pages relevant to your point. Use a semicolon between year and page numbers.

10. For an electronic document, name the medium and give enough other information for readers to find the item and read it for themselves. For a Web file, give the full URL (online address).

PRACTICAL TIP

Basic Formula for Numbered-List System (Vancouver Format)

IN YOUR PAPER

Book	(number)
Article	(number)

IN YOUR "REFERENCES" LIST

Book	number.	Lastname Initial. Title of book. City: Publisher, year; firstpage-lastpage.
Article	number.	Lastname Initial. Title of article. Journal title; volume(month): firstpage-lastpage.

CHAPTER 3

THE ESSAY: A Way of Exploring Ideas

Organizing ideas is always a challenge. Besides knowing your own processes of thinking and writing, it's helpful to know what your readers expect from specific types of documents. This chapter and the next two outline the usual expectations for the main types of documents that students write—starting with the most common assignment, the essay.

The ***essay*** *is a flexible and varied form. In fact, the word* essay *is derived from the French word meaning "attempt." The defining factor for an essay is that it considers ideas in some depth: it's a meeting point for writer and reader to try out some thinking together. Essays also make connections between your ideas and what others have already written on a subject. The book review, or critique, is a special kind of essay that concentrates on showing how a specific source can contribute to thinking on a topic.*

Organizing the Essay

To hold the reader's attention and respect, essays need to be well organized, but they can't just follow formulas or their ideas will die from lack of fresh air. This section focusses on ways to create strong but flexible structures for essays and reviews. The guidelines it gives are not rigid requirements, but descriptions of the ways things are usually done in North American academic cultures. They are meant to be adapted to specific assignments.

Thesis and Argument

Readers expect any essay to make a point, not just collect facts or scatter reflections. Academic essays, at least in North America, are usually organized around a **thesis**—a central assertion with which others may agree or disagree, and that can be explained and supported by evidence. It's in that sense that essays are often called **arguments**.

A statement of the thesis usually appears early in the essay. Though we don't advise trying to write the whole introduction before you have completed the body of your essay, it's a good idea to write out your planned thesis in a sentence or two early in the process. (See the entry on focus statement, page 9 in Chapter 1.) Some people put the thesis

The Special Case of Essays Analyzing Literature or Art

Don't force your ideas into an argumentative mould if it isn't suitable. In essays of literary or artistic analysis, for example, the central point doesn't necessarily have to be argumentative. It can be an interpretive idea that pulls together everything you say, a key insight that unifies your other ideas. In that case, your reader may not expect—or want—to have the central point stated outright until you have finished setting out your detailed analysis of the work. Check with your instructor if you're in doubt about where to position that overall interpretive statement.

statement on a card and keep it in front of them while they draft. Try that tactic as a way to keep your overall purpose in mind, but be ready to revise the statement as your ideas develop.

Characteristics of a Good Thesis Statement

To show that your discussion will be worthwhile, your thesis statement should have these qualities. (Note that the better examples use course concepts to improve the focus of initially weak versions.)

1. It is exact enough to focus your discussion.

✗ Dull, vague Grass is important in the African savannah.

✓ Precise, leads to an explanation Grass is the essential element in the African savannah's system of nutrient recycling.

✗ Weak, evasive The Anaconda Company has a problem with its accounting system.

✓ Dynamic To solve its problem of financial control, the Anaconda Company needs to adopt a fully computerized accounting system.

2. It is limited enough to be covered in the space and time available.

✗ Evidence not within reach I want to see if evolution is true.

✓ Can be tested My hypothesis is that the trait of dark wings in fruit flies can be changed within 20 generations by restricting the larvae's exposure to light.

✗ Unworkable The Democratic Party will always be strong in the southern states.

✓ Manageable Support for the Democratic Party in the southern states increased after 1960 when voters began to define their interests in terms of social class.

3. It is unified, so it can control a coherent discussion.

✗ A mere list The Loriaki site contains six kinds of pottery.

✓ A synthesis All styles of pottery at the Loriaki site combine simple forms and highly decorated surfaces.

Devising Your Introduction

The first paragraph or two of an essay ask your reader to join you in looking at a subject. Typically the introduction indicates the topic, scope, and method of reasoning you will use. Its style and tone also show your attitude. A bald statement like "this essay will discuss" doesn't sound as if you're eager to begin, and it isn't very inviting to the reader. Similarly, a list of points to be covered lacks dynamism. Here are some alternative ways of catching your reader's interest and signalling your intentions.

1. The Funnel Opening

In this standard opening, supply a backdrop that puts your topic in perspective. Step back a bit so you can lead to your specific area of discussion. Typically, you can end the paragraph with your focus or thesis statement. But note that many instructors are tired of this kind of opening. It works best when you have something essential to say about the context of your topic—perhaps (as in the example quoted below), to indicate that your paper will deal with a small part of a larger topic. Avoid huge generalities, which may sound forced and insincere.

2. The Thoughtful Disagreement

Outline what two or three other writers have said about your topic, and then state your own thesis. Such an opening signals a paper of argument, as well as indicating the context and scope of your topic. Be accurate and respectful of the opinions you cite, so that your own point seems worth exploring as an alternative.

3. The Quotation

This opening works particularly well when the quotation is from a person or work you will be discussing. Quote only a sentence or two to evoke some of the issues and questions you will deal with, and then move on with your own commentary. In literary essays, such a quotation may be printed as an epigraph, indented and single-spaced just under the title. In that case, you do not need to comment immediately.

4. The Question

A thought-provoking question can make a strong opening if it is truly relevant to your topic. It's best to frame a difficult or challenging question, one that needs some space to explore and requires weighing of alternative answers. A simplistic question or one with an obvious answer could kill the reader's interest from the start.

5. The Anecdote or Telling Fact

Journalists use this lead to grab their readers' attention. It may be suitable for some of your less formal pieces. Be sure that the anecdote or fact is directly related to the rest of your essay. Dictionary definitions or biographical facts are poor ways of using this tactic—they look like mere filler.

6. The Evocative or Intriguing Detail

A related approach is to cite a telling detail from the literary work, historical event, or problem situation that you will discuss. Here again, you want to indicate that your discussion will illuminate the kind of detail you cite.

PRACTICAL TIP

When to Write the Introduction

Don't think you need to get the introduction perfect before you can proceed with writing the essay. A good focus statement (page 9) may get you through, allowing space for exploration of possibilities. Or you can always write a preliminary introduction and then revise it to reflect what you actually said. Some people write the introduction last, drawing the map after they've seen the territory. In any case, revise your introduction carefully once the paper is finished, ensuring that it illuminates the path the reader will take, and that it works well with the conclusion.

7. The Blunt Thesis

In a short paper or exam answer, you may be wiser to have no introduction at all. Just start with a thesis statement and develop it. Used confidently, this can be the most satisfying opening of all, as long as your style is concrete and precise.

SAMPLE INTRODUCTION
(funnel pattern)

The society that Shakespeare depicts in *King Lear* is based on a hierarchy of power. Both the staging and the language of the play show that each character is in a specific position in the hierarchy, one of either authority or subordination. Each is either king or subject, father or child, rich or poor. However, some characters are aware that their social positions are roles or guises. When they alter or "dis-guise" their roles, their actions cause social chaos and raise questions about human relationships. The various disguises in the play, especially in Acts 3 and 4, show how fragile a social system is when it is built on this kind of role-playing.

Developing the Body of Your Essay

The main, middle section of your essay need not follow a rigid pattern of organization. But it does need to lead the reader smoothly through the material. And it should visibly display your own thinking, not just be a summary of information or a retelling of events.

Here are some ways to think about the body of an essay:

- It **analyzes** ideas: that is, it breaks down your topic into components and looks at each in turn. An essay about a poem, for instance, could discuss various poetic techniques; an essay in economic history would examine the factors that contributed to a historical situation. In this way you demonstrate your command of the methods of thinking used in your discipline. (See pages 9–13 for a list of the kinds of analysis commonly requested in academic assignments.)
- It also **synthesizes** ideas, bringing together the components you've looked at separately, and shows how they interact. The essay about a

poem would show how the poetic techniques contribute to the poem's central effect; the one in economic history could indicate how a crucial factor started a chain of events that led to the situation you're examining. Be very specific about what that central effect is, and the mechanism and outcome for the chain of events. You are expected to show some originality when you synthesize ideas, creating new ideas out of old.

- In an essay of argument, the body may need to **explain the thesis** stated in the introduction. It could comment on meanings of specific words or concepts you have used, perhaps indicating how your viewpoint is unlike ordinary ways of looking at the topic. A preliminary explanation is especially important when you are asked to write about a theory.
- It also **demonstrates and tests the thesis or central point**. This is where you use the data that you have been gathering through library research or the notes you've been making from readings. The body of the essay is the place to go into detail, offering relevant facts and discussing the meanings of passages. Keep relating this material to your overall point or thesis. If some facts are lacking to make a firm case, or certain elements don't fit your interpretation, say so. That will show your respect for complexity—a hallmark of essay writing.

PRACTICAL TIP

What to Do If Your Essay Is Too Short

What if your essay is too short? Widening the margins or spacing the lines farther apart isn't the answer. And padding your style will just weaken the impression you make. But here are three easy ways to develop your ideas:

- Give more examples or include more details.
- Include exceptions—then explain them.
- Outline different opinions from yours, and then comment on them.

Setting Out Your Conclusions

Readers expect essays to round off ideas at the end. That's not to say that a conclusion should be elaborate. In a short piece, when you have finished what you set out to say, you can often just stop. For a longer essay involving several ideas or a complex line of argument, it is good to provide a sense of closure. And since the final impression is often the most lasting, it's in your interest to finish with some verve.

The following are some common ways of organizing conclusions:

1. The Inverse Funnel

Restate the thesis in different words and then discuss its implications. Beware, though, of just repeating what you said at the beginning. Suggest, if you can, how your discussion has illuminated larger issues you have already mentioned. Don't add new ideas suddenly—your reader will wonder why you didn't discuss them in the essay.

2. The Full Circle

If your introduction is based on an anecdote, a question, or a startling fact, complete the circle by referring to it again here. Show how some of the insights in your essay have illuminated it or expanded its meaning.

3. Ending with a Bang

Some of the most successful conclusions end on a strong stylistic note. Vary the sentence structure—if your sentences are long and complex, try making the last one punchy and short, or vice versa. Or dramatize your idea with a colourful image, striking phrase, or quotation. This may also be a place to allow yourself a personal note. Show some of the excitement you've generated in your own thinking.

SAMPLE CONCLUSION
(using all of the above elements)

The theory of environmental determinism, as presented in the books by Steiner and Ruprecht, is inadequate as a basis for understanding native land claims in the sub-Arctic. The case of the Inuk in Charters Strait

> demonstrates its weaknesses, which all come from reliance on Western ways of thinking. Because it assumes that only "objective" evidence such as DNA testing can show who lived in the area historically, it will never be accepted by the native people themselves. Because it relies on the concept of cultural evolution, it cannot recognize the problems in the old policies requiring the Inuk to adapt and "catch up" to white society. The recent remark by a federal government official that the Inuk of Charters Strait "just need more housing to turn them around" (Smith, 1996) is an example of the oversimplified views that this theory tends to encourage.

The Critique, Book Review, or Book Report

Since academic learning depends so much on responding to what other people have written, you will often be asked to write a review or critique about specific books or journal articles. This is a time to read with special care and awareness. Follow the guidelines set out in Chapter 2, pages 29–31, to focus your attention on your own reading process. The assignment may vary from a simple summary of a work's contents to a sophisticated analysis and evaluation. Here are some guidelines for the two most common types, with notes on possible variations.

The Informative Report or Summary

A summary, or précis, can be a piece on its own, or it can form part of a larger essay or report. Your purpose is to replicate the contents of the source briefly, accurately, and coherently. This task calls on your ability to get to the heart of things—to separate what is important in terms of the course from what is less essential or useful. Think of yourself as writing "crib notes" for other students in your class who have been unable to read the work.

In creating a clear summary:

- Plan the length ahead of time.
- Give the same relative emphasis to each area as the author does.

- Follow the same order of presentation, making exceptions when necessary for clear reading.
- Indicate the logical chain of the author's arguments, indicating especially the author's thesis and the main topic sentences.
- Mention the key evidence supporting the arguments. Give examples only if you have space.
- Use your own words and sentence structures in preference to paraphrasing the source closely.
- Read and revise your summary to make sure it's coherent. (See pages 103–105 on paragraph coherence.)

If you are writing the summary as a separate piece, you may not need to give page references for each idea. But do identify the source piece by listing its full author and title, its place and date of publication, and the number of pages. Format this note according to the appropriate referencing system for your discipline, as set out in Chapter 2, pages 35–53. Separate the note from your discussion by three blank lines.

The Analytic Review or Critique

An analytic review or critique summarizes the main ideas in a book or article, and also shows how the author's argument is constructed. Begin with an introduction giving the overall effect of the piece, then follow with a summary of its main points and a commentary on them. You may also be expected to include some evaluation. Publication details can be given in an entry either at the beginning or at the end.

- **Introduction** Provide basic information about the nature of the work to prepare the reader for your analysis of its ideas. Some questions to answer:
  - What exactly is the work about?
  - What is the author's purpose? What kind of audience is he or she addressing?

    - What are the author's background and reputation? What other books or articles has he or she written?
    - Are there any special circumstances connected with the writing of this work?

- **Summary** Check with your instructor what proportion of your review should be devoted to outlining the work's contents. As in the simple summary discussed above, focus on main ideas and structure. For organizing your review, one choice is to present a condensed version of the work, followed by your analysis and evaluation. Alternately, you may integrate summary and analysis, assessing the author's ideas as you present them.

- **Analysis and Evaluation** As you read and plan your piece, ask yourself these questions; answer at least some of them in your writing:
    - How is the book organized? What logical pattern does it follow?
    - What assumptions does the author make, and are they valid?
    - What kind of evidence is presented to support the author's ideas? Is it reliable and up to date? Is the author's position convincing?
    - Does the author agree or disagree with other writers who have dealt with the same material or problem?
    - What does the work contribute to the overall topic of your course?
    - Does the book accomplish what it sets out to do? Are there any omissions, weak spots, or contradictions in the arguments?
    - Is the work clearly written and interesting to read?
    - Does the work raise issues that need further exploration?
    - To what extent would you recommend this book, and to whom?

Remember that your main focus is the argument of the book or article, not the information it gives. Thus the topic sentences of your paragraphs should keep saying "The article demonstrates" and "The uthor argues," rather than "The French Revolution developed" or Louis then decided."

)ther Kinds of Reviews

ometimes you will be asked to write a variation of the review paper.

If you are asked to give a *personal response* as part of your paper, ıen feel free to use the pronouns *I* and *my* and express your feelings bout the work. But as in any academic paper, back up your personal tatements with reasons and analysis.

When you are dealing with many works, as in the *literature review ection* of a longer paper, avoid discussing them one after the other in string. Instead, group them by subtopic and organize your discussion ıto those groupings. Thus your paragraphs would start with sentences aming the subtopics ("Hydrotherapy is an effective treatment in two pecific conditions"), rather than repeating monotonously "Jones iscusses hydrotherapy.... Lee also discusses hydrotherapy."

diting the Essay: Special Concerns

ince the essay and book review forms aim at drawing the reader into kind of discussion, write and edit them with readability in mind. While our word choice should be fairly formal (see pages 111–113) and you vill probably avoid using the pronoun *I*, you don't have to aim at ounding authoritative or imposing. Write as if you were engaged in a lass discussion with the instructor and other students whose opinions ou respect.

As in editing other forms of writing, begin with organization and ork on the finer points of grammar and style afterwards.

This checklist of editing questions focusses on the characteristics ıat readers hope for in essays. Combine some questions and overlook thers, depending on your strengths and weaknesses as a writer. If peer diting is encouraged for your assignment, ask a fellow student to give n opinion on two or three of these questions too.

1. Does the essay have a **main point** and state it explicitly? Does match what the assignment asked for? (See page 3 in Chapter 1 c understanding the assignment, and pages 55–56 above on the thes statement.)
2. Does the essay give adequate **explanation, evidence, and example** Does it use course concepts to analyze material? Does it give attentio to opposing arguments or evidence?
3. Are all sections **relevant** to the topic? Are the connections clear?
4. Does the essay show how its ideas are related to the **reading** yo have done? Does it use the documentation format expected? (Se Chapter 2.)
5. Do the **paragraphs** group ideas satisfyingly? Do paragraph breal and topic sentences signal shifts of focus? (See Chapter 6, page 103–105.)
6. Do **sentence structures** reflect the key relationships among ideas? A the words clear and exact? (See Chapters 6 to 8.) Are details lik spelling and punctuation correct enough so they don't distract th reader? (See Chapter 9.)
7. Is the essay **attractive in appearance**? (See page 23 on gener expectations of format.)

A personal checklist based on your known strengths and weakness can be even more useful than this general set. If your instructor admire your clear language last time, try for the same kind of clarity again. If yo have a weak area—irrelevant details, run-on sentences, pretentio words—give it special attention so it doesn't detract from your strength

CHAPTER 4

THE REPORT: Thinking About Facts

Reports are the basis of scientific communication, and are also common in business and the professions to convey the results of observations and studies. Readers of reports expect information and analysis they can rely on. They expect a report to be reasoned and orderly, so they can grasp its essential features quickly. They also want material that is precise and to the point.

This unit will advise you on the specific requirements for organization and style in the two main types of reports:

- *The* ***science report****, typified by the lab report often assigned to students, and sometimes adapted for papers in the social sciences*
- *The* ***business report****, written by students in management and other professional studies as practice for an important form of workplace writing*

The Lab Report

This basic form of scientific report follows a similar careful structure in all disciplines and throughout the world. It presents information so that anyone reading it or trying to duplicate the procedure would be likely to reach the same conclusions.

In a lab report, you explain scientific procedures rigorously but concisely. You can assume that your instructor is familiar with scientific terms, so you don't need to define or explain them unless requested specifically. However, you must set out your procedures, give details of your findings, and justify your conclusions, even if they are not new to the instructor.

Structure

The list below sets out the components expected in a lab report, showing the order they usually take. But don't think you need to write the sections in this order. You can't write the abstract until everything else is done, and the title and the introduction need only be put down in rough form until you see just what interpretive points you want to make in your concluding sections.

Except for the title page, use these terms (or combinations, such as *Materials and Methods*) as headings for the sections of a lab report:

1. Title Page
2. Abstract
3. Introduction
4. Materials
5. Methods
6. Results
7. Analysis
8. Discussion
9. Conclusion
10. References

1. Title page

Include the title and date of the experiment, your name, the date of submission, the name of the course and the instructor's name. Make your title brief but informative. Avoid empty phrases like *A study of* or

Observations on. Just state *what* you are studying—for instance: "The effects of ventilation on the attention span of classroom students."

2. Abstract

The **abstract** (sometimes called *summary*) appears on a separate page following the title page. It summarizes the purpose of the experiment, plus its method, results, and conclusions. A simple experiment may require only a few lines, but even for a complex one, keep the abstract under two hundred words.

A fully informative abstract answers the questions: Why did you do this study or project? What did you do, and how did you do it? What did you find? What do your results mean?

Here are some pointers for writing a good abstract:

- Make the abstract complete enough to stand on its own.
- Summarize your conclusions as well as the other sections of your report.
- Do not refer to information that is not in the document.
- Avoid using *I* or *we*. Use active verbs rather than passive whenever possible *(the study tested something* rather than *something was tested by the study)*.
- Give final figures rather than calculations. Avoid using abbreviations or unusual symbols. You would need to explain them, using up your word limit.

3. Introduction

Here you give the purpose or objective in more detail. If your purpose is to test a hypothesis arising from a particular problem, then state clearly the nature of both the problem and the hypothesis. (Be sure you don't give away your results—just state the idea you tested.) Include the theory underlying the experiment as well as pertinent background data. You may be asked to include a literature review to indicate that you have read relevant background material or comparable studies (see pages 62–65 on writing a review). Summarize the relevant ideas as concisely as possible.

4. Materials

This section lists the materials and equipment you used and gives some explanation of how you set up the experiment. (If the *Materials* description is short, combine it with the *Methods* section, forming a single *Materials and Methods* section.) If you need to use more than one arrangement of equipment, provide a full list of the equipment here, and then in the *Methods* section describe each setup separately before noting the accompanying tests.

Some departments require you to specify the source or supplier of any reagents you've used. Do so briefly, saying something like "Formaldehyde solution, 40% concentration, PDQ Chemicals." It may also be useful to specify the purity of a chemical by indicating "99.9% pure" or "ACS reagent grade."

Use simple diagrams to help the reader visualize physical operations. If you use more than one, give them titles and numbers. Diagrams work best integrated within this section, but for a student lab report, you may be allowed to put them on separate pages at the back. Hand-drawing is acceptable. Be sure you refer in the text of your report to any diagram you use, naming it by number and location.

5. Methods

This section sets out the procedures step by step in the order in which you actually performed them. Include enough detail to enable others to reproduce the experiment easily. If you followed lab manual instructions, you may not need to copy them out—simply refer to them and give details of any deviation. If a procedure is long, complicated, or not necessary to a full understanding of the experiment, describe it at the end of the report in a labelled attachment.

Be concise in your description of method, but don't omit essential details. If you heated a liquid in a test tube, report its temperature and how long it was heated. Note whether it reached its boiling point, for instance. Readers must know exactly how to perform the experiment themselves.

Ordinarily, you will describe the experiment in the past tense as a completed action ("Two of the males displayed some courting behaviour"). Increasingly, however, instructors may ask you to write this section as a set of instructions. In that case, use imperative verbs ("Cut off 2 cm from bottom of stem").

6. Results

This section will contain mostly measurements and hard data, with some preliminary calculations such as the averages of any operations you perform repeatedly. In student reports, you will usually present all your data, though you can look for ways to make them understandable and concise. Accuracy is crucial here. Your test of the hypothesis depends on it.

- Ask your instructor whether you should give the details of your calculations or just their results.
- Pay special attention to units of measurement, since omitting or misusing them is a serious scientific mistake.
- Where possible, include the uncertainty in the calculated values you report. You might, for example, report that a temperature is 21.0° C ± 0.3° C.
- For any calculations, check to see whether you should include statistical measures such as standard deviation, standard error of the mean, or coefficient of variation.

Summarize your results in graphs or tables wherever possible. See pages 85–87 for more detailed advice on setting up figures.

7. Analysis

Here you begin to show your reasoning about the data you have gathered. Take the data from your results and develop them further by more detailed calculations. Also use words to point out comparisons, trends, and changes. Look for surprising or unexpected results and draw attention to them. Make sure your graphs and tables focus on these patterns.

If you have been asked to keep the *Analysis* section separate from the *Discussion* and *Conclusion* sections, don't go beyond showing observable patterns—point out that the water took three times as long as the gasoline to evaporate, for instance, but don't try to explain why.

This is also the section where you may be asked to show your **error analysis**—that is, your awareness that your measurements are not absolutely accurate. For instance, when you calculate force using the formula $F = ma$, you need to calculate the range of uncertainty in F caused by the measured errors or uncertainties in m and a.

8. Discussion

In this section you interpret the results of the experiment and comment on their significance in the light of the experiment. Though often short, this section displays your ability to reason scientifically. If possible, compare the results of your analysis with theory or models. Note and explain any discrepancies.

Show *how* and *why* the experiment produced its outcome (whether expected or unexpected), and discuss the *factors* that influenced the results. You may also indicate where *further work* needs to be done to produce a fully trustworthy answer to the overall research question. In deciding what points to include in this section, try to answer the following questions:

- Do the results reflect the experiment's objective? Was your hypothesis confirmed or negated?
- Did the experimental method help in accomplishing the purpose of the test?
- Do your results agree with previous results as reported in the literature on the subject? If not, how can you account for the discrepancy? What—if anything—was different, and why? What was the source of the difference(s)?

- Could the results have another explanation from the one you have made?
- What further work could be built on your results?

9. Conclusion

This is a simple statement of what can logically be inferred (that is, concluded in the careful way of inductive reasoning) from the experiment. Use the present tense. Don't think you have to sound as though you have found all the answers to the scientific problem. Your phrasing here may still have to be tentative and limited: not "This experiment proves" but "These results suggest."

10. References

List the sources of any published information or ideas you have used. You may be asked to list books and journal articles in separate subsections. Be sure that your entries are complete enough that your reader could find and read the same items. For referencing format, consult your assignment sheet, and see also pages 35–53.

Editing for Scientific Style

Although the basic principles of revision and editing (see pages 20–22) are the same as for any other kind of writing, scientific writing poses some special challenges. Readers expect clarity and precision—they need to be sure they know exactly what you mean. Some common stylistic habits can weaken your presentation. Follow these principles:

Avoid Using Clumps of Nouns as Adjectives

Original	Adult male liver malfunction
Revised	Liver malfunction in adult males

Choose Verbs Instead of Abstract Nouns

Original	The **addition** of saline solution and subsequent **agitation** of the mixture resulted in the **formation** of crystals.

Revised (passive verb)	When saline solution **was added** and the mixture **shaken**, crystals **formed**.
Revised (active verb)	When we **added** saline solution to the mixture and **shook** it, crystals **formed**.

Avoid Vague Qualifiers

Be exact rather than depending on suggestion. Delete words like *quite, very, fairly, some,* or *many*. When possible, give specific measurements and make comparisons when relevant.

Original	The star was **much** brighter on 8 August.
Revised	The star was brighter **by 2 magnitudes** on 8 August compared with 6 August.

Use Active Voice as Much as Possible

You may prefer the passive voice for describing methods and results, but stick to active verbs in the *Introduction, Discussion,* and *Conclusion* sections—unless your instructor has directed otherwise.

Original (passive verb)	**It was suggested by the test** that subjects respond more quickly to negative stimulus.
Revised (active verb)	**The test suggests** that subjects respond more quickly to negative stimulus.

Avoid Ambiguous Pronouns

Original	To root, the cutting requires water. **It** must be warm.
Revised	The **water** must be warm.
Revised	The **cutting** must be warm.

Field Notes

In many areas of study, you will use **field notes** to record observations for further analysis and research. The field notes may then become part of another paper or stand on their own as an assignment.

Recording Systematically

In most cases, you will make your field notes by hand, so you need to be organized ahead of time. Make your notes accurate and consistent. Stick to what you actually saw, heard, smelled, or felt physically.

1. The First Page

Record at the top of the first page the purpose of your study, any key questions or hypotheses, and an outline of the methods you intend to use. Note the start date of your project and leave a space to fill in the completion date later.

2. Format and Structure

Your instructor may give you a particular format for recording field notes. The following arrangement is typical:

- At the start of each day, begin a new page with the date and time at the top. Divide each page into two columns. Use the narrower one on the left for headings such as location and time. Use the wider column for recording your specific observations.
- Be selective. Don't try to record everything you observe. The nature of the research question will help you plan what you need to observe, measure, and record. You may even be able to set up columns for the types of data you expect to record (for example, "soils," "slope," "land use").
- Be precise in noting the time and location of observations. Give locations in terms of the coordinates of a topographical map if you have one, or refer to approximate distances from permanent markers such as buildings.
- Give exact details in standard units (distances in metres, the number of tadpoles in a litre of water, temperature in degrees Celsius). Also indicate how you measured them if there is any possible ambiguity ("counted in full bucket," "oral thermometer 2 min. by watch").

Measure more than once if possible so you can calculate uncertainties later.

- Record your field observations consistently. If you record data one way at one site and another way at another, they may be useless.

Illustrations

The saying "A picture is worth a thousand words" certainly applies to field work. Use sketch maps when suitable, and drawings or photographs of the scene or of the equipment you see being used.

- A sketch map may be adequate if the scale is not critical. Sketch maps are easy to do, since they are only approximate recordings. If there is no time to take accurate measures, use the length of your own pace as an indicator ("five paces from shoreline"). Include an approximate scale, necessary labels, and an arrow indicating North.
- Similarly, for drawings, don't worry about drawing skill—with practice your work will be quite adequate to record essential information. Record only the essential features. Label important details as you go, or fill in labels soon after your visit.
- Take any photographs close enough to isolate the subject (unless you intend to show it in relation to other features) and be certain the details you want are clear. Make a list for yourself to record what pictures you are taking.

Summary Statements

Summarize your observations periodically, preferably at the end of each day. Reflect on what you have done that day and on your major observations while they are still fresh.

Reporting Field Assignments

In some cases you will be asked to turn in your original notes. More often, you will use them as the basis for a formal report. If your instructor simply tells you to "write a report on the field assignment," with no further elaboration, don't take this as permission to turn in a rambling, unstructured piece. Analyze your data and follow the structure for a lab report (see pages 68–73), presenting your observations and analysis concisely and systematically. Be sure to state in the conclusion whether your original purpose or hypothesis has been fulfilled.

The Business Report

Like scientific reports, business reports are based on the careful gathering of data, but they focus more on drawing practical conclusions. You may be asked to write a report of this kind in some social science or professional courses as well as in management studies.

Types of Business Report

Although in the workplace you will often write **routine informational** reports, as a student you are more likely to write **analytic** reports. These are the more challenging kind, because they go beyond collecting information and try to solve problems by analyzing situations. Responses to case-study assignments are often reports of this kind, as are many research reports.

If you need to write a **short report** of either kind, say two or three pages, set it up like a memo, with the standard *Date/To/From/Subject* headings. Divide the body into sections with a heading for each. Number pages other than the first. Short reports often use informal conversational language.

Your courses will probably assign **long formal reports** so you can develop your ability to be thorough and analytic. Such reports use a standard set of main headings—such as *Background, Discussion of Findings,* and *Conclusions* or *Recommendations.* They avoid personal pronouns and conversational style. Here are some characteristics of the long formal report:

- The sections often have subsections, with more specific descriptive headings.

- The pages after the first are numbered.
- A title page provides a formal cover.
- A table of contents guides the reader to pages of interest.
- An **executive summary** or abstract stands by itself at the front—a one-page highlight of the report's main ideas. It's easier to write after completing the rest of the report.

Optional components include a letter of transmittal, that is, a covering letter or memo providing the extra personal touch; one or more appendixes containing information that would slow the reader down if it were in the main text, such as added tables or summaries of raw data; and a bibliography that lists published or unpublished documents used in preparing the report, and sometimes people contacted in the research.

Choices in Organization

There are two methods of organizing the long formal report.

In most North American workplace situations, **direct** or **deductive order** is increasingly seen as the most efficient way to present your ideas. Since your report addresses a problem or a question, give your answer early—before your explanation of how you reached it. Like the thesis statement of an argumentative essay, the first section gives an assurance that the pages ahead have a point to make. You can use this basic order with any length of report.

- Summary (optional, depending on length)
- Introduction
- Conclusions and/or Recommendations
- Findings (data and observations)

However, some traditional organizations—and some traditional instructors—may prefer **inductive** or **scientific order**, wherein you set out data or findings (like the *Results* section of a lab report) before giving the conclusions or recommendations. This pattern also works well in the workplace when the reader may be displeased or skeptical about what you are going to say. It builds gradually toward the conclusions or recommendations.

Summary (optional, depending on length)

Introduction

Findings (data and observations)

Conclusions and/or Recommendations

In whatever order you arrange the sections, use each one for a specific purpose.

Here are some pointers on preparing the long formal report:

Title From the start, create a clear picture of your territory. "A Study of Ground Transportation" is too vague. "A Cost-Benefit Analysis of Three Options for Municipal Ground Transportation" is more precise. If your reader already knows that you will be doing a cost-benefit analysis, "Three Options for Municipal Ground Transportation" is more compact.

Introduction Begin with a brief statement of purpose. This may be a single sentence outlining the topic and indicating the action or solution foreseen: "This report recommends ways to increase the security of e-mail messages." In a long report, your introduction will probably also include more about the context or reason for the report, and may outline the method used to gather information. This is also the place to identify your assumptions. If you have limited the topic, tell why. Also say what factual assumptions you are making—that the supply of oil will stay stable, for example.

Conclusions or Recommendations Informative reports state conclusions generalizing from the observations. Analytic reports also give recommendations for action. If there are a number of conclusions or recommendations, list them, with the most important first. Don't be reluctant to state them so early in the report: your readers need to know that your work has arrived at usable results.

- ***Presentation of Findings*** Here you show how the facts or the data you have gathered lead to your conclusions or recommendations. Give as much data as your reader is likely to want. In the workplace readers are often happy just to have you summarize data, present it graphically, or indicate that it is available on request. For an academic paper, however, your instructor will probably want a substantial demonstration of your research. As with scientific reporting, indicate any sources of uncertainty in measurement.

To organize this section of the report, you may need several subheadings. In general, rely on order of importance. Start with the most important finding and give the details—perhaps the main cause of the problem that you are about to solve. Then make new sections and headings for other findings. If your report makes a list of recommendations, you can make each one the basis of a section.

You will probably use one or more of these principles of reasoning to set out your ideas:

- ***Classification and division*** You organize by factor type, such as fixed costs and variable costs.
- ***Cause and effect, or means and end*** You deal with each problem in turn, showing how it arose and how you propose to fix it.
- ***Spatial order*** You move from one location to another.
- ***Chronological order*** You trace events, moving from past to present to future.

Effective Editing

As with other complex writing tasks, your revisions will be more effective if you begin by looking at organization. For business reports, ask yourself these questions:

PRACTICAL TIP

Editing for Objectivity

To ensure that your writing shows the objectivity of your work, substitute numbers and terms of measurement as often as possible for such mushy terms as *excellent*, *great*, or *improved*. You can set the "Search" function of your word processor to find any such words that you know are stylistic habits. Then insert numbers or proportions:

✗ **Subjective** Faber Products had a fantastic sales increase in 1997.

✓ **Factual** Faber Products had a 30% sales increase in 1997.

Mentioning specific people or other companies can have a similar effect, suggesting that you have considered real-world effects. Referring to expert authorities may also help establish a framework for your points.

✗ **Pushy** The company has got to shape up by trying something new.

✓ **Practical** The team leader Jack Chung confirms that line workers would welcome a change to inter-station shifting.

✓ **Sensible** Norfasco tried this system in its Ippewa plant in 1992-1995, and achieved a 21% reduction in downtime.

✓ **Solidly reasoned** Smith's study argues that the whole industry is undergoing a shift in its function within the U.S. economy.

1. **Is the report focussed?** Will the reader be able to state my central message in a sentence or two?
2. **Is the report complete?** Have I addressed all of the reader's concerns and questions? If I have not been able to provide some important details, have I explained why?
3. **Do the conclusions and recommendations fit logically with the findings?** Are there explicit links between them? Have I considered

all the evidence fairly? Would the reader be able to reach a different conclusion from the same evidence? Are my conclusions objective or do they reflect a personal bias?

4. **Are there any inconsistencies, contradictions, or ambiguities in the report?** Could the reader misinterpret any part of what I have said?

Now turn to the surface structure of your report—the grammar, punctuation, and style. (See Chapters 6 to 9 for specific advice on these matters, and see also the advice on scientific style, pages 73–74.) One particular need for business reports is **objectivity**. A report that reads as if it were free of personal prejudices and subjective opinion will have more influence than one that seems biased. Instead of subjective language that pushes readers to see things your way, provide firm measurements and clear reasoning.

Special Visual Effects

Readers want to skim through a report and see its essential structure, whether it's presenting scientific or business material. Even a student report should look like a report, not an essay. With computer formatting, you don't have to be an expert artist or designer to create good effects. Here are some basic principles.

Use Space Creatively

Don't cram—leave space between sections and subsections. Densely covered pages seem more forbidding than pages with spaces. Leave wide margins—at least 3 cm (1 1/4 in.) at the top and right side and 4 cm (1 1/2 in.) at the left side and bottom, as a way of framing the text. Leave space too around headings, lists, and visuals. Reports have far more white space than essays do, and they're easier to follow because of it.

Use Effective Headings

Each section and subsection of a report should have a heading. In business reports especially, and in science reports, headings can tell the story of the report so that a reader glancing through will know the sequence of reasoning.

1. Use High-Information Headings

In science reports, the brief standard headings such as *Methods* and *Discussion* (see pages 68–73 above) are good because they signal the careful building-up of data and then interpretation. But in business reports, make your headings and subheadings "high-information" whenever possible, especially in your presentation of findings. Specific nouns and active verbs help. Use very short sentences or point form, but don't just rely on abstract nouns. Note the difference between the following sets of subheadings from a business report:

Low-Information Headings	*High-Information Headings*
Effectiveness	Medication X Is Most Effective
Cost	Medication Y Costs Less
Side-Effects	Medications X and Y Have Different Side-Effects

2. Use Typeface for Emphasis

With word processors, it's easy to use **boldface**, *italics*, underlining, and larger typefaces for headings. But be careful not to overdo the variety.* For a clear and consistent approach, remember:

- Capitals provide emphasis, but all-capital text is hard to read. Save it for the main title.
- Underlining now looks old-fashioned. Boldface stands out better.

---

*For lively, practical advice on using any brand of computer to create handsome and readable pages, see Robin Williams, *The Mac Is Not a Typewriter* (Berkeley: Peachpit Press, 1990).

- Italics are harder to read than conventional typescript and therefore are best saved for a few words at a time.
- Frequent changes of font and typeface create a cluttered look. Stick to two or three variants at most.

3. Consider Numbering Your Headings

While shorter, informal reports need no numbering, numbered headings in longer documents allow for easy cross-reference and indicate the relative importance of sections and subsections. Older systems use a combination of numerals and letters, along with indentation and capitals, like this:

A. MAIN SECTION TITLE
  1. First Heading
    a. First subheading
      i. first sub-subheading
      ii. second sub-subheading
    b. Second subheading
      i. first sub-subheading
      ii. second sub-subheading
  2. Second Heading

Now many business reports use the decimal system developed for technical writing. Though cumbersome to set up, it provides a clear sense of the hierarchy of ideas. All headings are indented the same, but you can use capitalization and numbers to show the different levels:

1. MAIN SECTION TITLE
1.1 First Heading
1.1.1 First subheading
1.1.1.1 first sub-subheading
1.1.1.2 second sub-subheading

1.1.2 Second subheading

1.1.2.1 first sub-subheading in this section

1.1.2.2 second sub-subheading in this section

1.2 Second Heading

Use Lists

Vertical lists have visual impact and allow for quick comprehension. They're seldom seen in essays, but are essential for reports. Use a list to simplify material when you have more than three consecutive items or ideas.

- If a list becomes too long—beyond six or seven items—group some of the items to make a smaller list.
- Number the items if you will be referring to any listed items later in the report, or if you want the reader to follow the list as a sequence. Otherwise, introduce each item by a dash (—) or a bullet (•).
- Use parallel phrasing for all items in a list so that it makes sense as a set. (See pages 109–110.)
- If each item is a sentence, begin it with a capital and end with a period. Otherwise, use lowercase letters and no final punctuation. A semicolon at the end of each item is now considered old-fashioned and unnecessary.

Use Illustrations

Charts, graphs, tables, and other illustrations clarify information and reinforce points.* Design them to be simple and uncluttered. In most cases, you should integrate the illustrations with your text so that they make maximum impact. Supplemental information may go in an "Exhibits" section at the end or in an appendix.

*For a fascinating account of the historical development of graphs and other visuals (and also much good advice on using them), see these two books by Edward R. Tufte: *The Visual Display of Quantitative Information* (Cheshire, Connecticut: Graphics Press, 1983) and *Envisioning Information* (Cheshire, Connecticut: Graphics Press, 1990).

Introduce each illustration, stating its main point in words so tha
the reader knows why it is included and how to read it. Don't just repea
the information in the illustration: point out trends and comparisons

- If you use more than two or three figures, give them titles an
numbers such as "Figure 1" or "Table 3." (The term *figure* include
all illustrations except tables.)

- Use tables to allow cross-comparisons within a set of measurement
Your wordprocessing program can set up tables easily.

- Use graphs and charts to show changes over time or to make mor
dramatic comparisons of measurements. Computer graphics softwar
can create simple line graphs or elaborate bar charts. Careful han
drawing is also fine. Use ruled graph paper and pencil, then retrac
your lines in black ink. With or without a computer, follow thes
basic guidelines:
    - Use a scale that allows you to distribute your data widely on th
    page, but don't make the illustration larger than necessary.
    - Put the independent variable (the one you have manipulated) o
    the horizontal axis, and the dependent variable (the one yo
    measure) on the vertical axis.
    - Make the vertical axis about three-quarters the length of th
    horizontal axis.
    - Label the axes, including the units used (or use a legend on th
    side), to show the reader exactly what you have plotted on th
    graph.
    - Title and label the graph informatively (for example, "Figure
    Yearly Sales for 1995-1998") so you can refer to it by number
    your text.
    - Where possible, put error bars (±) on data points.

- Consider whether you should find a line of "best fit" to show the trend in your data. Ask your instructor for guidance if necessary.

SAMPLE FIGURE

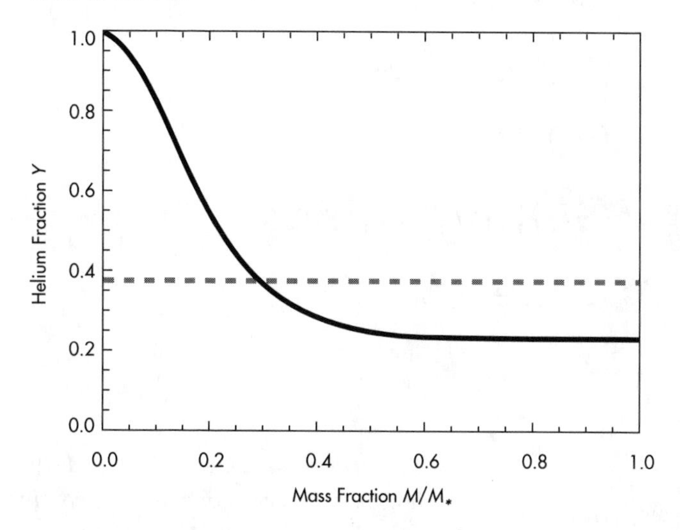

Fig. 1.—Helium profiles for two stars: a 1.6 $M_\odot$ unmixed star (*solid line*), and an initially fully mixed 1.6 $M_\odot$ star (*dashed line*).

Source: *The Astrophysical Journal,* December 1995; by permission of the authors, A. P. Sills, C. Bailyn, and P. Demarque.

C H A P -

OTHER PRACTICAL FORMS: Getting Things Done

This section discusses the structures and styles use in a few specific types of practical writing tha students often need to do. Again, the principles ar simple: knowing what you want to say, an understanding what readers expect from specifi kinds of presentation. As in the chapters on essay and reports, the advice and examples are meant to b adapted for different situations.

Proposals

A proposal is a written request for approval of a plan of action. There are two basic types, with varieties of each: an academic proposal and a business proposal. Like a report, a proposal focusses on practical considerations, and it also uses headings and other visual effects.

The Academic Proposal

An **academic proposal** is the first step in producing a thesis or major project. Its intent is to convince a supervisor or academic committee that your topic and approach are sound, so that you gain approval to proceed. The proposal usually contains these ingredients:

- A rationale for the choice of topic that shows why it is important or useful.
- A review of existing published work ("the literature") relating to the topic. Here you need to tell how your proposed work will build on existing studies, yet explore new territory.
- An outline of your intended approach or methodology. Depending on the subject, this may include costs, resources needed, and a timeline of when you hope to get things done.

People reviewing academic proposals are often experts in that field. They are likely to assess how clearly and thoroughly the proposer has thought about the topic and its potential problems as an extended project. Make sure, therefore, that the details you give are sufficient to present a good case for your proposal. Also make sure they are correct. In the review of the literature, for example, check that the bibliographic facts are accurate.

The Business Proposal

A **business proposal** may be a response to a formal request for proposals (an RFP) or it may simply reflect your own initiative—something you want to do that requires approval or funding. (Officers in student organizations often need to write such proposals. So do students wantin to set up business ventures of their own.) Discussed below are the typica elements you will need to include. Arrange them as separate section with headings and subheadings (see pages 83–85 on creating goo headings). In deciding how much emphasis to place on each, conside what is most likely to influence the decision-maker.

- A short **summary** of the whole proposal and the reason for it. Use well-constructed paragraph to set the context, showing how the proposa addresses a need. If the RFP already states the reader's need, sho concisely that your plan fulfills it. If you are writing an unsolicite proposal, take more space to define the need in terms the reader wi recognize as relevant.
- A **detailed outline** of your plan of action, including the methods yo will use. This section will probably fall into subsections, signalled b subheadings. It will set out a technical description of the service o product proposed. If possible, also try to include some method o evaluation or followup, building a sense of confidence in the advantage of what you are offering. Guarantees or routine checks are examples c such after-service selling points.
- A **timeline** giving the sequence of steps and the completion date You can effectively show this on a flow chart—a chart that plots th flow of steps, with dates for each stage.
- Your **qualifications**, and perhaps the names and addresses of peopl for whom you have done similar work. For proposals where th proposer's ability and experience are critical, you may want to includ a full résumé. If you will use other people in the enterprise, giv evidence of their qualifications as well, and indicate the lines c responsibility.
- A **review of costs**. Since the budget can be the vital ingredient in th success of a proposal, be as detailed as you can, especially if you proposal is in competition with others. It's helpful to put the cos breakdown in a table, for ease of discussion. If cost is not important t your proposal, at least indicate that your methods will be efficient rathe than wasteful.

- An outline of the reader's **benefits** from implementing the proposal. If your proposal is competing against others, outline what its special features or competitive advantages are—from the reader's point of view.

Organization and Style

Because of the practical function of most proposals, you can use business reports (as set out on pages 77–82 of Chapter 4) as your model for organization and style. Use headings, lists, and visuals to make reading and cross-referencing easy. The more objective and concrete your style, too, the more believable will be your claims about what you can do.

Common Weaknesses in Proposals

Since proposals compete with other proposals, be sure that yours bypasses the following common weaknesses. Readers will be glad that you have spared them yet another letdown.

FAULT	IMPROVEMENT
Not paying enough attention to reader benefits	Tell what will add extra value to your proposal—giving details that will show how the proposal fills a particular need.
Omitting some elements given by a written request for proposals	If you choose not to follow some details of the specifications, say why. Don't just avoid the issue.
Vagueness about cost	Be as precise as possible in providing cost figures, especially if cost will be a deciding factor in accepting or rejecting your proposal. If your budget can only be an estimate of cost rather than a fixed commitment, be sure to say so and give the reason.
Lack of enthusiasm	Use the introduction to indicate why you are interested in seeing the proposal implemented. Although a proposal should maintain a professional tone, a reader will more likely respond well to one that projects a sense of commitment rather than a seeming shrug.

Electronic Mail (E-Mail) Messages

As a student, you will often use e-mail as a means of communicating with your instructors as well as fellow students. In the workplace, it's replacing the print memo as the main form of communication within companies. Here are a few tips for making the most of this new form of communication:

- Create informative subject headings to catch readers' interest and get your messages read. Precise nouns, personal pronouns, and active verbs work miracles. Compare these examples:

Boring	Request for Information
Eye-catching	Where Can I Buy Your Product?
Easy to delete	Re: Your Mail
Worth reading	Answer to Your Question About Meeting

- Quote a few words of the original message in your reply to remind your reader what topic you're discussing. But remember that quoting more than this is a waste of disk space.
- Don't beat around the bush. As with any memo, the key to getting read is to put the most important idea at the start. Don't compose introductory sentences just for their own sake. What do you want the reader to do or know? Say so up front, and then explain.
- Be informal, but keep in mind your real-world relationship with the reader. If you aren't on a first-name basis with your instructor, for instance, stick to "Dear Professor [surname]" in the salutation. But at the end, take a few words to say something friendly: "See you next Tuesday" rather than "Sincerely yours."
- People don't mind a few typing errors and flawed sentences in e-mail. But make your message understandable—look it over before you send it.
- Be careful about your tone. If reading messages quickly, readers may take innocent jokes as anger or sarcasm. Try inserting some of th

following signals, known as **emoticons** (just look at them sideways) to help prevent misunderstanding. Note that they all indicate fairly weak emotion.

:-)	Smiley	"This is a joke"
;-)	Wink	"I don't really mean it"
:-0	Dismay	"I'm unpleasantly surprised"
:-(	Displeasure	"I don't like this much"

- Remember that e-mail messages are not really private. Don't write what you would be embarrassed to have others see.

Résumés and Letters of Application

Employers often receive hundreds of applications for a job opening. The person responsible for reviewing them will not want to spend much time reading each. In creating an application letter and résumé, therefore, be brief, precise—and interesting.

What to Say

A résumé is not just a summary of facts. It's a selling tool designed to show that your qualifications fit an organization's needs. You will need to supply some basic information, but how you organize it depends on what you want to emphasize. Put your most important qualifications first, so they are noticed right away. For most students this means leading with educational qualifications; for some, work experience may be more impressive. Use reverse chronological order, so that the most recent item is at the beginning.

Never claim more for yourself than is true; including a falsehood in a résumé can be grounds for firing. In most provinces and states, you are not required to say anything about your age, birthplace, race, religion, or sex. (Use of initials instead of your given name can hide the latter.) But if you feel it would be to your advantage to include any or all of these facts, do so.

Here are the kinds of information readers expect to see in résumé

- **Name, address, and telephone number** Use capital letters or bol face type and centre your lines at the top of the page. If you have temporary student address, state where you can be reached at othe times.
- **Objective** It's helpful to let the employer know either your caree goal or the kind of position you want. Or use a "Profile" subhead ing and summarize in a sentence or two the main benefits you brin to the work you are seeking.
- **Education** Include any degrees (including those you are still workin on) and related diplomas or certificates, along with the institutio that granted or will grant them and the dates.
- **Awards or honours** These may be in a separate section or include with "Education."
- **Work experience** Give the name and location of the employer, alon with your job title and the dates of employment. Instead of outlinin your duties, list your accomplishments on the job, using point for and action verbs. For example:

    Designed and administered a local marketing survey.

    Supervised a five-member field crew.

    Created a summer crafts program for disabled children.

- **Special skills** List here any information that may give you a advantage in a competitive market, such as experience wit computers or knowledge of a second language.
- **Other interests (optional)** Sometimes giving a few achievements interests, such as in athletics or music, will show that you are wel rounded or especially self-disciplined. Avoid a long list of items th merely show passive or minimal involvement.
- **References (optional)** If asked to supply references, give the comple title, address, and phone number of each. Check beforehand wit those named, as a courtesy.

The Traditional Form of Résumé

This is the kind you will use for conservative employers such as banks or government agencies, and can rely on for any entry position. It has a standard set of headings so that readers can easily compare one applicant with another, but it still leaves you some choice in how you fill in supporting information. Note how the point-form information in this example stresses the candidate's combination of practical experience with specialized academic training. This brief version could be adapted and expanded for specific positions.

JACK CHANG

Address until May 1998:
68A Marsh Road
Halifax, NS B3J 3J9
(902) 555-5081

Home address:
2345 Bondy Street
Coquitlam, BC V8T 3J9
(604) 555-0019

EMPLOYMENT GOAL

An entry position in interior design, where I can contribute my artistic knowledge and experience to challenging projects

EDUCATION

- BFA in Design Studies, Nova Scotia College of Art and Design, expected May 1998

HONOURS and AWARDS

- Dean's List 1995-6, 1996-7
- Fletcher Award as top student in Art History, 1997

WORK EXPERIENCE

Summer 1997 Decorating Assistant, Home Decor Co. Ltd., Vancouver

- Helped customers choose colours and fabrics for in-home decorating
- Assisted chief designer with sketches for large institutional project
- Prepared advertising brochure (enclosed) for drapery promotion

Summer 1996 Crew member, Painters Anonymous

Summers 1993-5 Assistant to Hank Rejoy, Inc.,
Furniture Re-upholstering, Burnaby

OTHER SKILLS, INTERESTS, and ACHIEVEMENTS

- Theatre set design: designed and created sets for three-act play, NSCAD March 1996
- Played 1996-8 for Schooners, inter-university soccer team

The Functional Résumé

If you are writing to an employer who will appreciate creativity an enterprise, consider a functional résumé. This structure also gives yo an advantage when your formal qualifications are not directly related t the position you want. Some functional résumés set out experience i different work roles (for example, Research, Administration, Sales) Others may focus on personal attributes such as initiative, teamwork communication skills, or analytic ability. They give enough specifi

REBECCA GOPNIK
18 River Street
Markham , Ontario L53 4J4
(905) 555-3020

JOB OBJECTIVE
Summer position as a guide for the Toronto Tourist Bureau.

PROFILE
Creative, bilingual individual with record of hard work and experience as a tour guide.

COMMUNICATIONS SKILLS
- B.A., Honours, in English, University of Toronto, expected June 1999; B+ average.
- Reporter, then features editor, *The Quad*, campus newspaper, 1996-8.
- Announcer, CTUP, campus radio, September 1996-present. Write and host two-hour weekly program on community affairs.
- Tour guide, University of Toronto campus, May-September 1997. Led small groups on two-hour walking tours of campus; chosen as guide for VIPs, Pan-American Free Trade Conference.
- Fluent in spoken and written French.

INITIATIVE
- Set up and ran campus "bike doctor" company, 1996-present. Supervise staff of seven making house calls, create print and radio ad campaigns; annual gross now $70,000.
- Ran pet-grooming business, 1993-5; made enough money to cover tuition for first three years of university.

REFERENCES
1. Professor Sarah Yan, University of Toronto, Department of English, Toronto, ON M5W 1B3, (416) 555-4658.
2. Timothy Bartlett, Director of Student Affairs, Wilson Hall, University of Toronto, Toronto, ON M5W 3B4, (416) 555-5698.

lata (including dates) to back up such claims. For a complex functional ésumé, it can be wise to include at the bottom a brief record of mployment, so that the reader knows when you did what. This sample f a functional résumé shows that the applicant is flexible and energetic s well as experienced in work related to the position advertised.

Having Résumés Ready

PRACTICAL TIP

Create two or three different kinds of résumés for the main types of pening you foresee, and then tailor them rapidly when a specific pportunity arises—an easy matter with computer formatting. For nstance, if you're undecided between marketing and sales, and could ven work at a daycare if you had to, organize your basic information or each of these possibilities, perhaps using a functional format for ne. Then update the appropriate version quickly when you need it.

Making the Most of Application Forms

PRACTICAL TIP

f you're completing an application form with set questions, fill it in to ain some of the advantages of a résumé. Among others done with less are, your form will stand out.

First, be complete. Putting in all the requested information not only eeps you from being eliminated for lacking a needed qualification, ut also shows that you're competent in processing information.

Think about arrangement. Emphasize the facts that put you in the best ght by placing them first in the set spaces and by giving more details.

Be as neat as possible, using consistently sized printing. Especially if ou can fill out the form at home, do a trial run in pencil so you can roduce a polished-looking final version in ink.

The Letter of Application

When employers open the envelopes you send, they should see an application letter first, and it should make them want to read your résumé. A good letter can even open the door to the next stage in job-seeking—the interview. Take the time to craft each letter to focus directly on the particular job and company. Show that you know something about the company and link your skills to the needs of the position.

One challenge in writing a letter of application is to tell about yourself and your qualifications without seeming egotistical. Limit sentences beginning with *I*. Instead, bury some *I*'s in the middle of a sentence where they will be less noticed (for example, "For two months last summer, I led a crew. . .").

Also, avoid making unsupported, subjective claims. Instead of saying "I am a skilled manager," say something like "Last summer I managed a $50,000 field study with five assistants." Rather than "I have excellent research skills," you could say, "Because of my work in his class, Dr. Clifford Barnes selected me from twelve applicants to assist in his summer research program."

Here's an example (don't copy it outright) of the body of an application letter that aims to connect the applicant's background with the needs of an employer:

> Your advertisement in the *Ottawa Journal* for a daycare manager caught my attention, since my qualifications match those you are looking for. As a graduating student in Early Childhood Education at Algonquin College, I would like to apply for the position and have enclosed a résumé.
>
> Besides my specialist academic program, I have had relevant child care experience that has equipped me for this position. For two summers I worked with Dr. Raymonda Bone of Carleton University Children's Centre, both caring for the children and planning the daily program. My part-time work as a research trainee at the Early Childhood Education Centre in Toronto also made me aware of management practices in this field. As a retail store manager for three years, I have also proven my ability to gain the respect of a diverse group of employees and to lead them effectively.

My résumé gives further details of my background and experience. I would appreciate the opportunity to discuss further with you how I might contribute to your daycare program, and will call you next week to discuss a possible interview.

Creating an Electronic Résumé

PRACTICAL TIP

Recently, applicants have begun to send documents electronically through the Internet, often to "résumé banks." Employers search these collections of résumés electronically to find people with the qualifications that match their needs.

Although these documents can't use sophisticated visual elements, you can follow the general guidelines for overall structure and design. Either the traditional or the functional format is suitable.

One addition is needed: a set of keywords at the beginning of the document, used to let employers search for specific qualifications. Be sure to use concrete terms for what you claim. Employers don't look for vague terms like "reliable" and "imaginative," but for particular programs of study, job titles, languages, and computer skills. Of course the body of the résumé then has to provide hard evidence that you have the qualifications mentioned.

Appearance and Presentation

Your application will be judged on how you present it as well as by what you say. The look of your page makes the first impression. Master the use of tabs and boldface, using lots of white space. Create a clear, professional-looking page so that the reader can find information readily. Computer programs can supply you with ready-made formats, but they may not be organized to create the particular emphasis you want. It's better to create your own plain but suitable page design. Also, take the time to double-check for spelling and grammar. Errors, especially in the address, salutation, or first paragraph, provide an easy way to thin out a pile of incoming applications.

Admissions Letters

When you are asked to write a letter or personal statement as part of an application to a college, university or graduate school, use the chance to interpret the facts about yourself already visible in your résumé and transcript. Write to show who you are and what you would contribute to the program.

Do Some Research

The first step is to read printed and online material from the program, and to seek out contacts with past and present students as well as faculty members. Find out what qualities and activities the program emphasizes—you will present yourself differently for a professional program that focusses on group problem-solving than for one that expects independent research. Note how the program defines its distinctiveness and successes, so you can indicate the relevance of your own interests and achievements.

Be Focussed

If you are given a list of questions to cover, examine them to find the "decision factors" by which candidates will likely be sorted. You may see clues suggesting concern about applicants' ability to withstand stress, distrust of their motives for applying, or interest in maturity or varied life experience. By looking for these underlying concerns, you will probably be able to group some of the set questions, covering a few main points about yourself rather than stringing out repetitive answers.

If you are asked simply to write a statement of interest or intent, include clear, concrete answers to these likely implied questions:

- What attracts you to this program?
- What have you done in the past that indicates you will succeed in it?

What can you contribute to the program or profession?

What do you intend to learn in the program?

What will you do with what you learn?

Be Coherent

how that the facts of your life hang together, displaying a sense of urpose or adding up to strengths of character. Back up your claims bout yourself by referring briefly to the facts listed in the other parts of our application ("As my academic record shows"), and offer enough xamples so that your letter could stand on its own. Discuss academic nd non-academic achievements together as evidence for what you ay about your character and interests. You may want to use an outline o plan coverage of your major points. In editing, look at your paragraph tructures to check that the reader can follow you from point to point.

e Personal

our letter substitutes for an interview. It is your chance to get readers o remember you out of the many candidates they screen. In effect, he readers have asked you to tell stories, comment on facts, and expand n selected details. It is also a place to mention points that might not how up in the rest of the application—your ethnic background or olitical interests, even, if they are relevant to the interests you will evelop in further study. Don't be afraid to mention problems or ifficulties; stress how you overcame them and say what you learned rom the experience.

Choose simple, natural language when discussing yourself and your ims. Use *I* rather than phrases like *this writer*. To avoid monotony, ou can start some sentences with a subordinate clause such as *While scrubbed floors* or *Because of my difficulties*—then go on to *I did* or *learned*.

CHAPTER 6

STRONG STYLE: Connecting to Your Reader

Depending on the purpose and reader, writing can have a range of styles. As a student, though, you will always benefit from being able to write in a style that is coherent, concise, and forceful. This chapter sets out three principles for achieving those qualities. They all involve attention to your readers' reactions. ***Paragraph structure*** *is a way to guide readers through units of writing, and* ***sentence structure*** *and* ***wording*** *keep readers interested in what you are saying. Our discussion in this chapter concentrates on the strengths you can gain by attending to these elements.*

)eveloping Coherent Paragraphs

Making your thought "flow" for the reader is almost as great a challenge s organizing your ideas. Paragraph structures provide a map for your leas, guiding the reader through your reasoning. If you have problems ulling your thoughts together, review this simple set of principles.

Jse Topic Sentences

xpress the central idea of each paragraph in a **topic sentence**. In xpressive and journalistic writing, this sentence can go anywhere in the aragraph—beginning, middle, or end—or it can just be implied. In cademic writing, however, the topic sentence nearly always works est at the beginning of a paragraph, stating the idea to be developed in ne rest of the paragraph. It lets the reader know what to expect. Don't ount on the people who read and grade your papers to guess what aragraphs are about, or even wait to be told—they're more likely to skip paragraph that neglects to make a point at the start. Note this exception: n the introductory and concluding paragraphs of essays and reports, opic sentences can safely come at the end.

xpand on the Topic Sentences

hink of the body of your paragraphs as developing what your topic entences state. You can **explain** more fully what you mean, giving efinitions or indicating distinctions. You can **offer details**, examples, r relevant quotations. Or you can follow through a **sequence**, showing ow one idea or fact leads to another through cause and effect, or occasionally) question and answer. All the ways of developing ideas n papers apply in miniature to paragraphs. See pages 9–13 for a handy st of the most likely patterns.

Use Appropriate Linking Tactics

Often the simplest words do the most to pull ideas in a paragraph together. **Pronouns** such as *it* and *they* and *this*, for instance, keep your focus on the ideas announced at the beginning of the paragraph—as long as they are clearly linked to the nouns to which they refer. **Deliberate repetition** of words also helps, as these paragraphs show:

> It's perhaps not surprising that Marshall McLuhan, the most influential **communications** expert of the twentieth century, was **a Canadian**. As a **nation**, **we** have been **preoccupied** with forging **communication** links among a sparse, widespread population. The old **Canadian** one-dollar bill, with its line of telephone poles receding to the distant horizon, illustrates **this preoccupation**. Year after year **we** strive to maintain a **national** radio and television broadcasting system in the face of foreign competition. **We** have been aggressive in entering the international high technology market with **our telecommunications** equipment.
>
> Nevertheless, while **we** have put **our** imaginations to work on the technological aspects of **communicating**, **we** still have a distance to go in recognizing the importance of **communications** on a day-to-day level. Business as a whole is just beginning to appreciate what the successful Japanese and North American companies have known all along—that excellence comes not only from technological know-how but from handling people well. Good managers are usually good communicators, whether the process of communication is systematic or informal.*

Certain **specialized linking words** can also be powerful tools for pulling ideas together. But don't just sprinkle them into your sentences—use them logically to support the ideas already present in your sentences. Usually the simplest words have the clearest logic. Here are the most basic functions, with a few examples:

---

* From Margot Northey, *Impact: A Guide to Business Communication*, 4th ed. (Toronto: Prentice Hall, 1997), p. 3.

'o Signal a Reinforcement of Ideas

also	in other words
in addition	for example
moreover	

'o Signal a Change in Ideas

but	on the other hand
however	instead
yet	in contrast
although	

'o Signal a Conclusion

accordingly	thus
therefore	so [*informal*]

PRACTICAL TIP

Jsing Sentence Subjects to Unify 'aragraphs

'o pull together paragraphs that seem to lack clear focus or energy, ry a **series of sentences with the same or related grammatical subject**. tart by underlining the subject of each clause. Then check to see if ou have stuck to two or three subjects consistently (nouns and their ronouns count as only one subject), and see if the shifts are appropriate. evise to reduce the number of subjects, so that you repeat the same ocus in a number of sentences before moving to another focus.

The sample paragraphs above use this tactic. Note how the first aragraph, once it has defined its topic as the Canadian attitude to ommunication, uses *we* as the subject of the final two sentences. The ext paragraph signals strong contrast by the word *nevertheless*, but it ontinues to use *we* in the opening sentence. Then it shifts the rammatical subject to *business* and *managers*. This special kind of epetition has led the reader through a large sweep of ideas and into he specific topic of the rest of the piece.

Vary Paragraph Length

A series of long paragraphs can make your writing seem dense and therefore difficult to read. Check any paragraph that takes a page or more to see if it would be better as two paragraphs. Look also for paragraphs only two or three sentences long, like those in newspapers and advertisements. They make academic writing seem disjointed or skimpy. Try combining a few short paragraphs into one around a single topic sentence.

Creating Lively Sentences

The first impression you make on your readers comes from the rhythm and structure of your sentences. A lively sentence has energy that almost pulls the reader through it.

Favour Active Verbs

In a sentence with the **active** voice, the grammatical subject *does* something to a receiver or object.

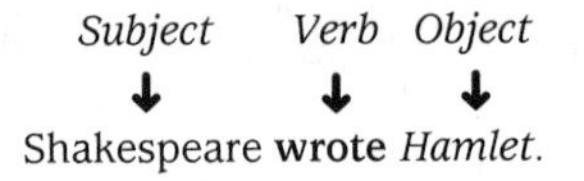

With the **passive** voice, the grammatical subject does not act but is **acted upon**.

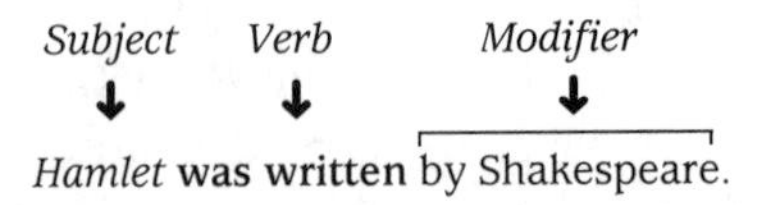

Why prefer the active voice to the passive? As the term itself suggests, the active voice is more dynamic. It also tends to make a sentence clearer and more concise.

Passive Voice	The lab report **has to be written** by the student in two hours.
Active Voice	The student **has to write** the lab report in two hours.

Note: Occasionally the passive voice is the better choice—but these onditions are relatively rare. Note that a number of them involve overing up something rather than expressing it directly—that's not an ffect you should try for very often.

. To indicate that the subject is literally in a passive position—is having something done to it.

    ✓ The statue **is being corroded** by acid rain.

. To avoid placing responsibility or blame, or to remain anonymous in narrating scientific procedures.

    ✓ The decision **was made** to raise student tuition.

    ✓ The muscle **should be massaged** lightly.

. To avoid an awkward shift of subject in your writing. In this case, the passive can help you maintain focus.

    ✓ Just as the instructor began the scientific demonstration, he **was interrupted** by a deafening explosion.

ary Sentence Length and Structure

eep your writing interesting by using sentences of different lengths, with mphasis falling in different places.

The easiest factor to control is length. Short sentences give emphasis nd are easiest to read. That's why newspaper writers use them so nuch. But strings of short sentences can seem choppy and may not how enough connections among ideas. For more sophisticated and moother writing, try out ways to **bring the ideas together**.

Choppy	Thomas Hardy wrote novels. He also wrote poems. Many people prefer the novels.
Smoother	Many people prefer Thomas Hardy's novels to his poetry.

A more common problem in colleges and universities is too many ong sentences. Long sentences can show complex relationships if andled well, but also easily lose direction and exhaust the reader. They end to weigh down student writing. See if you can split some of them and **recombine** ideas to show their real connection. Look especially for strings of main clauses joined by *and* or *then.*

Loosely Joined	The potatoes in the dark box grew an average of 3.2 sprouts each **and** the sprouts were pale green **and** they averaged 4.3 cm in length.
More Concise	The potatoes in the dark box grew an average of 3.2 pale green sprouts each. The sprouts averaged 4.3 cm in length.

Or combine sentences in such a way that one main idea stands out and the rest are subordinate to it, using **subordinating conjunctions** like *because, although, unless,* and *if.*

Disjointed	Clients may have specific dietary needs. You should arrange for special food preparation.
Smooth	**If** clients have specific dietary needs, arrange for special food preparation.

To decide what combination of long and short sentences is appropriate, **read your writing out loud** (or have someone else do it—and listen carefully). If you stumble somewhere because you have lost the sense (or the other reader does), chances are you should rewrite that sentence. With effective prose, you will feel a rhythm that moves you forward smoothly from idea to idea.

Make Major Ideas Stand Out

To make your main ideas stand out, subordinate minor ideas. Try out some of these patterns to find out which ideas are your main ones. Notice how an idea gains emphasis by placement at the end of a sentence—the next sentence will continue to develop it:

✗ Mary Ann Evans used the pseudonym George Eliot **and** she published *Middlemarch* in 1867. *[two unconnected ideas]*

✓ When she published *Middlemarch* in 1867, Mary Ann Evans used the pseudonym George Eliot. *[the main idea is the pseudonym]*

✓ Using the pseudonym George Eliot, Mary Ann Evans published *Middlemarch* in 1867. *[the main idea is the book's publication]*

Avoid *There Is* and *There Are* Beginnings

Although occasionally useful, these constructions more often take the energy out of a sentence. They use up one of the places for emphasis, and tend to create strings of other unimportant words.

✗ **It is**, some political theorists claim, the prospect of the nation state to wither away.

✓ Some political theorists claim that the nation state will wither away.

✗ **There are** specific species of plants that botanists recommend for pest control in gardens.

✓ Botanists recommend specific species of plants for pest control in gardens.

Avoid Long Chains of *Who* and *Which* Clauses

A sentence containing a series of clauses beginning with *which, that,* or *who* is often wordy and confusing. Split the sentence or look for ways to compress the wordiness.

✗ The women **who** worked in the munitions plant, **which** employed 300 people, enjoyed the contact with others **who** belonged to their age cohort.

✓ The women workers in the 300-person munitions plant enjoyed the contact with others in their age cohort.

Keep Phrasing Parallel

Give items in a series the same grammatical form. The rhythm adds clarity and emphasis.

✗ Socrates was **respected** by his associates, **admired** by his friends, and **his students loved** him.

✓ Socrates was **respected** by his associates, **admired** by his friends, and **loved** by his students.

✗ Pierre Trudeau **headed** the Canadian Liberal Party and also **campaigned** for a new Constitution. He **was a champion of** individual human rights too.

✓ Pierre Trudeau **headed** the Canadian Liberal Party, **campaigned** for a new Constitution, and **championed** individual human rights.

Using Exact, Plain Language

In most subjects you can think more clearly with ordinary words instead of fancy ones. What's more, readers prefer to read prose that makes sense immediately rather than requiring repeated readings. Most often, choose words that you would use in everyday speech and could read out loud without stumbling or feeling self-conscious. Unless you have a very good reason for using a long, fancy word, stick with the plain ones. (See pages 113–114 on the special case of technical language.)

FANCY OR COMPLICATED WORDS	PLAIN WORDS
commence	begin
determinant	cause
prodigious	huge
utilize	use
cognizant	aware
sufficient	enough
multiple	many
incremental	added
terminate	end
finalize	finish
modification	change

Be Reasonably Formal

You'll often hear that academic writing should be formal, but that doesn't mean it has to be full of long words or roundabout structures. It shouldn't be long-winded or boring either. *Formality* simply means that you are asking readers to take your ideas seriously—you're taking extra care with the *form* of your language. Here are some guidelines for academic writing.

1. Avoid slang

Slang words usually have short-lived or fast-changing meanings and may even mean different things in different regions. They're too inexact for academic writing. Dictionaries mark slang words as **nonstandard** or **colloquial**. Translate your intentions into more exact measurements (for example, "an increase of 37% over last year's sales" or "an average gain of 2.1 kg per month"). Note that putting quotation marks around a slang term does not make it acceptable in formal writing—it just confirms that you've avoided the need to find precise wording.

2. Use *I* Only When It Is Justified

For most academic writing, avoid *I* and *me*. In **essays**, phrases like "I think" or "I feel" suggest that your opinions are merely personal. You can often just delete those phrases. Instead, concentrate on making your interpretive statements precise and backing them up with evidence and discussion. Most **scientific writing** also avoids personal pronouns. Use impersonal style for most statements, omitting reference to the specific people who performed the action. For instance, you would say "The addition of baking soda to the mixture produced carbon dioxide gas" (instead of "When I added baking soda to the mixture, I made carbon dioxide gas"). Similarly, a social science paper might begin "This study analyzes three social factors contributing to homelessness" (rather than "My study analyzes three social factors contributing to homelessness").

However, occasionally using *I* or *we* makes the most sense. Ask your instructor if you think these **exceptions** may apply to what you are writing:

1. Use *I* where you are asked to relate personal experience, as in a journal entry or report where the reader will want to know your reaction (for example, "I noticed this connection only on reading the poem for the third time").

2. Use *I* occasionally to avoid roundabout or unclear sentences. For instance, "I conclude" is clearer than "It can be concluded."

3. In a few scientific procedures, the role of people is important. Thus, in a *Discussion* section, you might need to say "During the computer breakdown from 11:36 p.m. to 2:37 a.m. I visually observed 67 meteors." Many science publishers now encourage such personal references and active verbs ("I observed") because they give a more precise picture of the specific investigation.

3. Avoid Using *You*

Some informal prose (such as this book) addresses the reader directly. In academic writing, however, the word *you* may seem to point a finger at the individual reader, even where that's not intended. Instead, use inclusive terms like *people* or *everybody* if that's what you mean, or choose specific ones like *consumers, students,* or *North Americans*.

The pronoun *one* is also an alternative, at least for British-trained speakers of English. If you use *one*, remember not to lapse back into *you*. Check that your possessives also follow through: not *yours* or *his or hers*, but *one's*.

4. Use Few Contractions

Some people object to seeing written words shortened or run together the way we all do in talking. Writing out *it is* instead of *it's* and *cannot* instead of *can't* is one way of asking the reader for serious attention. Spell out technical short forms or acronyms the first time you use them. If you go to the trouble of saying "lower back pain (LBP)," then your reader won't be lost when you use *LBP* later in the piece.

5. Be Aware of Connotations

Word meanings include the feelings associated with words, as well as their denotations or literal references. Describing a person as *vigilant*, for instance, gives a much more positive impression than calling her *wary*, even though both mean "careful and watchful." Saying that an author *establishes* an idea indicates that you accept the reasoning, whereas saying that an author *claims* something leads into your argument against it. A thesaurus gives no guidance on these distinctions among similar words, but good print dictionaries do.

Control Jargon

Jargon is just technical language used inappropriately. When you write to another person in your field of study or profession, specialized terms can provide shortcuts for complex ideas. But even specialists say they get tired of seeing their colleagues' writing loaded down with technical words. The effects are even worse when you are trying to present technical material to non-specialist readers. Non-specialist readers are especially suspicious of jargon, thinking that bureaucrats, business people, and academics use big words to conceal meaning or cover up unpleasant realities—saying *rationalization* when they mean *firing*, for instance.

Here are some measures to prevent the bad effects of jargon:

- If you find yourself relying on long words one after the other, stop and restate the point in ordinary language. Even for your academic readers, clarity is more important than fancy phrasing.
- If many of your words end in *-ion* or *-ment* or *-ness*, convert them to verbs. Relying on verbs creates simpler, more forceful language.
- When you first use a technical term, provide a definition nearby. That practice shows that you have a clear sense of the concept yourself, and it helps ensure that you and your reader are both thinking of the same meaning.

> Jane Austen lived in **a world where male status and values were dominant**. Her thinking, however, was not entirely bound by this **patriarchy**.

- When you find the right term, use it consistently. Don't confuse your reader just for the sake of elegance. If you decide to use *Paleolithic*, for instance, don't switch back and forth between that and *Old Stone Age*.
- When it's necessary to use long words, keep your sentences short—perhaps twelve or fifteen words on average. Magazines like *Scientific American* use that principle to help intelligent readers process complex ideas.

PRACTICAL TIP

Using Readability Scores

In some areas of North America, laws require "plain language" in insurance policies, bank loans, and government regulations to ensure that the public can understand them. The laws sometimes specify **readability scores**, based mostly on average lengths of words and sentences. A figure for **grade level** summarizes these scores.

The "style-checkers" and "document information" commands of wordprocessing programs can calculate approximate readability scores for what you write. For clear academic writing, try to keep the average word length around five letters, the sentence length below fifteen words, and the grade level around twelve. That would put your writing into the same category as high-class newspapers and magazines. Don't try to create prose as heavy as that of your textbooks, which often weigh in with a grade-level score of over 20. (The text in this box has an average word length of five letters, an average sentence length of sixteen words, and a grade level of 11.5.)

Avoid Clichés

Colourful or emphatic phrases often get so overused that they lose all interest and meaning. Although many clichés were once expressive metaphors, their literal meaning has been forgotten because of overuse. In writing, they sound thoughtless and mechanical. (*Cliché* is the French word for "click," as in a wooden stamp being used again and again.)

Some rules of thumb:

- If you can complete a phrase when you've just heard the beginning, chances are it's overused. It's probably also wordy.

  worked like a ___ window of ___

  wear and ___ last but ___

- Check that metaphors make sense in your context. Don't risk sounding silly.

  ✗ Thatcher was **pumped up** for her speech.

  ✓ Thatcher spoke **enthusiastically**.

  ✗ These species of pine were ill-suited for a northern climate, but they **gave it their best shot**.

  ✓ These species of pine were ill-suited for a northern climate, but **they adapted by growing laterally and developing thicker needles**.

- Give a good expression a new twist. If a cliché fits what you want to say, try extending it, the way clever advertisements do.

  ✗ Mixed metaphors — The **cascade** of investors **flocking** onto the floors of stock exchanges **gave rise to** an enthusiastic **bull market** that continues to **run** at a **torrid** pace.

  ✓ Amusing comparison — The investors **flocking** to buy shares are **like sheep obeying the farmer's dog**.

Edit Out Wordiness

Nothing annoys readers more than wordiness. Seeing words with no value makes them feel cheated. Much of your revising will consist of making your style more concise. If you can recognize and get rid of common wordy patterns like these, your writing will gain in force and readability.

1. Prune Out Intensifiers and Qualifiers

Words like *very* and *many* attempt to add emphasis, but usually weaken the word they modify. Most can be cut or replaced. If you know you have the habit of using one of these, use the "Search and Replace" command of your word processor to find them. Usually you can just delete and let the other works speak for themselves. Sometimes you will need to give more exact measurements.

very, really, extremely, definitely	[just delete these]
a considerable amount of, to a certain extent	[give a more exact measurement such as *57%* or *until* December]

2. Thin Down Padded Verbs

Turning plain active verbs into wordy verb-plus-noun phrases may seem more dignified, but it creates flabby wording. Check especially *-tion* or *-ment* endings and see if a lively verb is buried there.

Instead of	*to have an expectation*	use	*to expect*
Instead of	*to make a decision*	use	*to decide*
Instead of	*to make an inquiry*	use	*to ask*

3. Shun Formula Phrases

Inflated phrases like these are equivalent to clearing your throat before starting to speak. Replace them with simpler terms or delete them.

Instead of	*due to the fact that*	use	*because*
Instead of	*at this point in time*	use	*now*
Instead of	*basically*	[delete it]	

4. Reduce Redundant Words

In conversation, we tend to emphasize an idea by doubling it. In writing, this habit sounds pompous. Strip the phrase to the essential word.

Instead of	*future prospects*	use	*prospects*
Instead of	*consensus of opinion*	use	*consensus*
Instead of	*return again*	use	*return*

5. Delete Unnecessary *To Be*

These words can be deleted when they serve no essential purpose in the sentence. Sometimes you can get rid of passive voice this way too (see page 106).

Weak	This method is considered **to be** accurate.
Improved	This method is considered accurate.
Even Better	This method is accurate within 0.005 mm.

Be Specific

To show your reader that you know what you're talking about, prefer exact, concrete words to vague generalities. Give numbers whenever possible, and when you use a generalization, supply an example to bring it to life.

✗ General, boring	It was a hot summer.
✓ Leads into analysis	Average daily temperatures in June and July 1997 were 2° C above the 100-year average for those months.
✗ Vague, sweeping	Crime is increasing in King's County.
✓ Worth hearing about	Convictions for violent crime in King's County increased by 10% over last year. Residents were particularly alarmed over the rise in murders from three to five.

CHAPTER 7

STANDARD GRAMMAR: Making Things Clear

You already know the main principles of grammar. You use them to make yourself understood in ordinary life. You say "Please pass me the salt" without stopping to wonder why you're saying me, *not* I, *or why it's* pass, *not* passes. *When you're writing, however, there are times when you do interrupt your work or come back to it, wondering about such things.*

To succeed in academic writing and in the workplace, you need to master ***Standard English****. That's the variety of English based on the preferences of educated people over the last couple of hundred years. It's now expected and considered "correct" in written documents among different countries and many cultures. Some of its patterns come from the* *gic of sentences; others are more arbitrary. And even Standard English hanges over time and from one region to another.**

This chapter covers the points that academic readers are most likely consider flaws in Standard English. It can't stand alone as a guide to good riting, but the things it covers are essential to being taken seriously as writer.

especting Sentence Boundaries

hree frequent flaws in sentence structure are easy to fix: the **sentence agment**, the **run-on sentence**, and the **comma splice**. They all come om misjudgements about what makes a complete sentence.

entence Fragment

sentence fragment lacks a crucial element. The omission may be eliberate, as when you say "Here!" in answer to a question, instead of am here." Deliberate fragments, where the missing part is easy to upply, are common in advertisements, but in academic writing they ound too casual.

An unintended fragment is a non-sentence, and the lack of completion auses frustration for the reader. It often occurs because writers leave ut a main verb or confuse a subordinate clause with a main one.

---

o make a study of usage in general, or to look up detailed advice on specific problems, you can consult ecialized guidebooks. Three different types are (1) *The American Heritage Book of English Usage: A actical and Authoritative Guide to Contemporary English* (Boston: Houghton Mifflin, 1996), which measures andard "rules" against the preferences of professional writers; (2) Don LePan, *The Broadview Book of ommon Errors in English*, 2nd ed. (Peterborough, Ontario: Broadview Press, 1992), which makes clear, thoritative judgements on right and wrong usages; and (3) the *Collins Cobuild English Guides* (London: arperCollins, various years), a set of small books based on current usage in the United Kingdom. They explain oblem points for second-language learners, including prepositions and articles.

✗ Napoleon's final defeat, losing the battle of Waterloo.

✓ Napoleon's final defeat was losing the Battle of Waterloo.

✗ Although he redrafted the last act of the play.

✓ Although he redrafted the last act of the play, it still did not please the audience.

Run-on Sentence and Comma Splice

A run-on sentence isn't just a long sentence, but one in which the writer has neglected to create a join between one clause and another. A comma splice isn't much better: the writer has put only a comma between the clauses, thus "splicing" them loosely. These patterns neglect to provide a clear signal of the relationship between the clauses. They give the impression that the author isn't in control of the flow of ideas.

What Is a Sentence?

A sentence names something and then puts it into action or shows it in relationship with other things or ideas.

When you're wondering if your words form a real sentence, check first that they contain these two components:

1. A **subject**, that is, a person or thing or idea that is the central focus. It will be a noun (*Montreal, Luther, table, justice*) or a pronoun *(it, she, somebody*).
2. A **verb**, that is, a word expressing action or a state of being or relationship. The verb will have a form that matches the subject (singular or plural?) or the time (past, present, future?).

Then check whether your subject-verb set can stand independently. If it starts with subordinating words (such as *although*, *because*, or *if*) or relative words (such as *which* or *that*) make sure that it goes on to complete the idea—or see if in fact it belongs with the sentence before it.

You can correct either of these faults in several ways. Note that each correction gives a slightly different emphasis and sense of connection.

Sentences with Flawed Structure

✗ Run-on She completed her first novel in one year it took her four years to write the second one.

✗ Comma splice She completed her first novel in one year, it took her four years to write the second one.

✗ Comma splice She completed her first novel in one year, however it took her four years to write the second one.

Possible Corrections

- Divide the two sentences with a **period** or a **semicolon**.

  ✓ She completed her first novel in one year. It took her four years to write the second one.

- Connect the sentences with a **coordinating conjunction** (***and, or, nor, but, yet, for*** [in the sense of *because*], ***so*** [in the sense of *and therefore*]).

  ✓ She completed her first novel in one year, **but** it took her four years to write the second one.

- Subordinate one clause to the other with a **subordinating conjunction** (***although, as, because, if, when, where, who, which***).

  ✓ **Although** the actors rehearsed two hours a day, they learned a new play every week.

  ✓ The actors, **who** rehearsed two hours a day, learned a new play every week.

  ✓ **Although** she completed her first novel in one year, it took her four years to write the second one.

  ✓ This novelist, **who** completed her first novel in one year, took four years to write the second one.

- If two main clauses are closely connected in thought, use a **semicolon** between them. (See pages 156–157 on the semicolon.)

  ✓ She completed her first novel in one year; it took her four years to write the second one.

PRACTICAL TIP

Using *However* and *Therefore*

Students often rely on the adverbs *however* and *therefore* to join clauses. These words are useful in academic reasoning, because they indicate the common logical patterns of contrast and causation, respectively. Unfortunately, they are not coordinating conjunctions like *and* or *but* and cannot (in Standard English usage) serve by themselves to join main clauses. Using a comma with them only creates a comma splice.

Run-on sentence	✗ **The crop failed therefore the price of wheat shot up.**
Comma splice	✗ **Handel wrote many operas, however Bach wrote none.**

The easiest way to mend this particular error is to insert a semicolon between the clauses:

✓ **The crop failed; therefore, the price of wheat shot up.**

✓ **Handel wrote many operas; however, Bach wrote none.**

But don't overuse this construction. It sounds very formal, and can become monotonous. Other options for joining sentences signal the logical relationships just as clearly and more smoothly:

✓ **Because the crop failed, the price of wheat shot up.**

✓ **Handel wrote many operas, but Bach wrote none.**

Maintaining Subject-Verb Agreement

It's only logical that the subject and the verb of a clause should agree in number. Obviously, single subjects take single verbs, and plural subjects take plural verbs. But that principle often gets lost in long or complex sentences. Here are some danger points and ways to handle them.

Pitfalls in Subject-Verb Agreement

1. Wide Separation of Subject and Verb

Mistakes often occur if the main word of the grammatical subject is a long way from the verb. Make a point of checking for subject-verb agreement when your sentences have to be constructed this way. But also look for ways to shorten the distance between subject and verb.

✗ The **time** spent on a full year's worth of space experiments **were** wasted when the equipment malfunctioned.

✓ The **time** spent on a full year's worth of space experiments **was** wasted when the equipment malfunctioned.

✓ The **year's work** on space experiments **was** wasted when the equipment malfunctioned.

2. Compound Subjects

Subjects made up of various components operate differently depending on the way the components are related. *And* adds subjects together, so a plural verb is needed. *Or* (and its negative form *nor*) refers to the subjects separately, so the verb agrees with the part closest to it. Check your sentences with that basic distinction in mind.

✗ The sociologist **and** the historian **is** right on this point.

✓ The sociologist **and** the historian **are** right on this point.

✗ Neither the sociologist **nor** the historian **are** right on this point.

✓ Neither the sociologist **nor** the historian **is** right on this point.

✓ Neither the sociologist **nor** the two historians **are** right on this point.

Note as well that certain joining words and phrases do not create a compound subject. They give the sense of a "rider" rather than an addition to the subject. If you use words like these, make the verb agree with the noun that constitutes the real subject, not with the "rider."

along with	as well as	in addition to	together with
including	like	for example	such as

✗ Library Science 500, **as well as** Bibliography 501, **are** required in the Masters program.

✓ Library Science 500, **as well as** Bibliography 501, **is** required in the Masters program.

✗ The Russian army, **including** the conscripts from the Ural region, **were** approaching the Chinese border.

✓ The Russian army, **including** the conscripts from the Ural region, **was** approaching the Chinese border.

3. Collective Nouns

A noun referring to a group—such as *family, jury, orchestra*—can have a singular or a plural verb, depending on whether the subject is referred to as a unit (singular verb) or as a collection of individuals (plural verb). Think about the intended logic when you write your sentences.

✓ The jury **were** escorted to **their** respective hotel rooms. [The word *jury* is *plural* in this sentence, because each member of the jury is considered individually.]

✓ The jury **has** rendered **its** decision in record time. [The jury acts as a *unit* and is therefore considered singular.]

4. Special Pronouns

The words ***each, every, everybody, everyone, nobody, someone, somebody,*** **etc.** (technically called *indefinite pronouns*) are plural in meaning but singular grammatically. To maintain Standard English usage, remember that they mean "one at a time." Often you can avoid problems by using a plural noun instead.

✗ Each of the factors **are** present in this case.

✓ Each of the factors **is** present in this case.

✓ All of the factors **are** present in this case.

Note: Although British custom uses a plural verb with ***none***, American usage requires a singular verb. Canadians get a choice!

✓ British **None** of the factors **are** present in this case.

✓ American **None** of the factors **is** present in this case.

Dealing with Verb Endings

PRACTICAL TIP

If English is not your first language, you may find that you keep making errors in verb endings, especially *-s* and *-ed*. Here are a few strategies for lessening the frustration.

- Use deliberately simple short sentences for a while as you develop skill and experience. The subject-verb problem (and others) will diminish when you can easily see the essential structure of your sentence.
- Try reading your work out loud—and listen to what you say. Most learners manage such details better in speech than in writing, so you'll likely find a few more errors yourself.
- If you're faced with a problem sentence, try using a "tag question" to check. Read through your sentence, then tack on "doesn't it?" or "didn't they?" at the end. Chances are that you'll choose singular *it* or plural *they* correctly. Then see if the verb matches what you've chosen.

Avoiding *He or She*

PRACTICAL TIP

As well as requiring singular verbs, indefinite pronouns take singular pronouns—and since they refer to people, that means you have to keep using *he* or *she*. That's awkward and wordy. Increasingly, even in Standard English, the plurals *they* and *their* are accepted after such words as *everyone* and *someone*. To avoid possible objections, however, you would be better to use a plural noun instead. *People* will often substitute nicely, or you may be able to be more specific with a term such as *children, all my friends*, or *most teenagers*.

Verbs: The Forms They Take

Verbs change their form to give precise shades of meaning. Besides those that indicate singular or plural subject, the other main changes are in **tense** or time reference (past, present, future?) and **voice** (active or passive? [see page 106]). There are lots of possibilities. The simple verb "to move," for instance, can take all these forms to make a simple statement with the subject *they*. (Other verbs don't take all these forms. Some verbs take irregular forms.)

TENSE	ACTIVE VOICE	PASSIVE VOICE
Present	they move	they are moved
Present Progressive	they are moving	they are being moved
Present Perfect	they have moved	they have been moved
Simple Past	they moved	they were moved
Past Progressive	they were moving	they were being moved
Past Perfect	they had moved	they had been moved
Simple Future	they will move	they will be moved
Future Progressive	they will be moving	they will be being moved (rarely used)
Future Perfect	they will have moved	they will have been moved

Verbs also change form for other functions—for instance, giving orders (the imperative) or naming unlikely possibilities (the subjunctive). Here are a few, again with the verb "to move" in active and passive voice:

Imperative	Move! [subject *you* implied]	Be moved!
Subjunctive	If they moved,	If they were moved,
	If they had moved,	If they had been moved,

Combining Verb Forms

The use of verb tenses and moods challenges anyone writing in English. It's not only that using the right verb ending can be tricky, but also that you need to combine various verb forms within sentences and paragraphs. Watch for the following problem areas.

Sentences with *If*

With the tiny word *if*, you can describe imagined situations while making clear that they are just imagined. But to do so, you need two kinds of verbs in each sentence. To indicate an *unlikely possibility*, you need specialized forms of the verbs—one kind in the *if* section and another (using *would*) in the consequence section. (Don't use *would* in both clauses.)

✗ If I **would have learned** Russian, I **would be able** to understand the Russian news.

✓ If I **had learned** Russian, I **would be able** to understand the Russian news.

✓ If Hamlet **were** more direct, he **would court** Ophelia more convincingly.

Note: Increasingly, British-trained writers use the simple past tense instead of the subjunctive ("If Hamlet **was** more direct, he **would court** Ophelia more convincingly"). But in North American writing, you should still use the subjunctive, as shown above.

Relating Past Actions to Other Past Actions

To show that one past action is further in the past than another event, use the *past perfect tense* for that verb.

✓ The developers **bought** three motels in 1994, even though they **had lost** money on the six they **had bought** in 1990.

✗ The retired history professor **said** that he **wrote** numerous monographs during his twenty years as a teacher.

✓ The retired professor **said** that he **had written** numerous monographs during his twenty years as a teacher.

Writing About Literary Works

Use the **simple past tense** to refer to a literary work in its historical context.

✓ Charles Dickens' *Oliver Twist* **was** a revolutionary work for nineteenth-century society. Dickens **used** it to criticize the harsh Poor Laws of his time.

But favour the **present tense** to discuss what happens within a book or work of art. That usage suggests that the work can still "speak" to us.

✓ The scenes of poverty and juvenile crime **are** still powerful today.

✓ In the next scene, Hamlet **sees** the funeral of Ophelia and **displays** his grief by jumping into her grave.

Use the **present perfect** tense (*has* or *have* plus the past participle to indicate that an event has taken place before the event you are discussing. (This tense, however, is less used in the United States than in other countries.)

✓ Hamlet **is** only mildly repentant after he **has stabbed** Polonius.

✓ Hamlet **is** only mildly repentant after **he stabs** Polonius.

Maintain the present tense even when you quote words in the past tense:

✓ "I **took** thee for thy better," Hamlet **says**.

Keeping Pronouns Clear

Pronouns are convenient because they can take the place of bulkier nouns. You don't have to keep saying *the test tube* or *Jacobean playwrights* when you can substitute *it* or *they*. But some patterns of use can cause slight blurring of meaning, tiring readers out because they have to keep guessing what is meant.

1. **Make sure the pronoun's meaning is unmistakable.** Watch out for places where it might be misunderstood, and try different wordings to bring the pronoun and noun closer together. You may need to repeat the noun instead of using a pronoun.

   ✗ The **beaker supply** in the lab had run out, so we borrowed **them** from the storeroom.

   ✓ The **beaker supply** in the lab had run out, so we borrowed **beakers** from the storeroom.

   ✓ Because the lab had run out of **beakers**, we borrowed **them** from the storeroom.

   ✗ The faculty recommends longer class hours along with more frequent tests, but students are protesting **them**.

   ✓ The faculty recommends longer class hours along with more frequent tests, but students are protesting the **longer hours**.

2. **Use *it, this,* and *which* to refer to specific nouns, not just general ideas.** Sometimes you will need to insert a noun or rephrase to avoid using a pronoun.

   ✗ The second division of the army was showing signs of unrest, confusion, fatigue, and hunger. **This** led to a mutiny.

   ✓ The second division of the army was showing signs of unrest, confusion, fatigue, and hunger. **This combination** led to a mutiny.

   ✗ Lawrence was a keen observer of nature, **which** shaped his poetry.

   ✓ Lawrence's keen observations of nature shaped his poetry.

3. **Check that your pronoun agrees in gender as well as number with the noun for which it substitutes.** You may have a problem if the gender is not specified. Using *they* to refer to a singular noun is one way out, but it's not yet acceptable for most academic work. Using plural nouns throughout is usually the best way to avoid problems, or you may be able to recast to avoid pronouns altogether. See pages 138–140 on unbiased language.

✗ When **a student teacher** begins in the classroom, **their** performance should be closely monitored.

✓ When **student teachers** begin in the classroom, **their** performances should be closely monitored.

✓ The performances of beginning student teachers should be closely monitored.

Consider using *one*. British writers often do, though the usage is less common in Canada and the United States, where it can seem too formal. If you do use *one*, be consistent. Don't mix *you* and *one*.

✗ If **one** were to carry out the experiment, **one** would run into so many side issues that **your** concentration would be severely affected.

✓ If **one** were to carry out the experiment, **one** would run into so many side issues that **one's** concentration would be severely affected.

4. **Make clear whether any personal pronoun is functioning in the sentence as subject, object, or possessor.** (See pages 164–165 on possessive forms.) Written Standard English demands more exact distinctions than informal oral language.

Personal Pronouns: The Forms They Take

SUBJECT	OBJECT OF VERB OR PREPOSITION	POSSESSOR
I	me	mine
you	you	yours
he	him	his
she	her	hers
it	it	its
we	us	ours
you	you	yours
they	them	theirs

To be formally correct, the pronoun should take the **subjective** form whenever it is the subject of a clause. Often, though, that usage is so different from spoken English that it sounds pretentious. If in doubt, reword to avoid the problem.

✗ James Thurber wrote "The Secret Life of Walter Mitty." It was also **he** who drew the famous *New Yorker* cartoons of the timid man and domineering woman. *[correct for writing, but stiff]*

✓ James Thurber wrote "The Secret Life of Walter Mitty." **He** also drew the famous *New Yorker* cartoons of the timid man and domineering woman. [*correct and more natural-sounding*]

The pronoun takes the **objective** form if it is the object of a verb or preposition. That principle applies even where the object may not come immediately after the verb or preposition.

Object of Verb

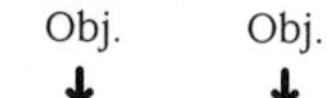

✓ The course evaluation criticized both Brooks and **her**.

Object of Preposition

✓ The duties were divided between **them** and **me**.

Two points to watch for:

When the preposition is followed by a clause, the pronoun takes the form required by its position in the clause. Often it is a subject, and so takes the subjective form.

✓ The audience was curious about **who** would speak the epilogue. [*not* whom, *because the pronoun is the subject of the verb* speak]

In certain comparisons, pronouns take the subjective form even where they may look like objects, because they're actually subjects of understood clauses.

✓ He's a better athlete than **I**. [not *than me*, because the pronoun is the subject of an understood clause *than I am*]

PRACTICAL TIP

Choosing Between *Who* and *Whom*

Who is the subject form of the pronoun, while **whom** is the object form. There is a growing tendency to use *who* rather than *whom* in speech and informal writing, but for academic writing it's safer to use *whom* as the object form. Here's how to choose the appropriate form.

In Standard English, use *whom* in two instances:

1. As **object of a verb**:
   - ✓ Many of the soldiers **whom he commanded** admired him.
   - ✓ The voters did not know **whom to blame**.
2. As **object of a preposition**:
   - ✓ The electors **to whom** he had sent gifts still failed to vote for him.

   - ✓ Never send to know **for whom** the bell tolls.

T E R 8

THE RIGHT WORDS: Adapting to Fit

his chapter will outline some of the standard atterns of word use, looking especially at readers' xpectations about the types of words that fit ifferent situations. If you can develop a sense of the vays words gather their meanings from their ontexts, you'll be able to make your own choices nore confidently when you enter new and different ircumstances.

Since people who are learning English as a new nguage are often puzzled by the broad range of ords available, we will give special attention in this hapter to the challenges they face (watch for the on shown in the margin here).

Increasing Your Vocabulary

English has a huge range of words, many borrowed and adapted fron other languages. As the main language of twentieth-century trade anc science, English has also invented words to keep up with nev developments.

Invest in Reading

The only sure way to enlarge your mental store of words is to rea regularly. Read what interests you—newspapers and magazines ar fine if they keep your attention better than heavy books. Reading out lou with friends can be a good way to reinforce your sense of the wa words sound together, as well as being a chance to discuss the subjec matter.

Don't interrupt your reading to look up every hard word. Mar unfamiliar words for later review if necessary, but make "educate guesses" as you go. Often you can find explanations nearby. Analyze th structure of new or hard words. Where the word is long and technica search for a central part (often from Greek or Latin) containing the basi meaning; then see how the added parts have created a more specifi meaning.

anthropology	comes from	*anthropos* human + *logos* thought
geology	comes from	*ge* earth + *logos* thought
geography	comes from	*ge* earth + *graphein* write

Once you start to notice these patterns, especially with technical word you will be able to remember words' structures and make out ne combinations even at first sight.

anthropomorphic	comes from	*anthropos* human + *morphe* form
geomorphology	comes from	*ge* earth + *morphe* form + *logos* thought
graphology	comes from	*graphein* to write + *logos* thought

Make Words Your Own

You can **reinforce your discoveries** by writing out a few key words from each reading session. Mark up each word for structure, and say it aloud to bring in your sense of hearing (the dictionary will guide you on pronunciation). Note where you first encountered the word, and watch for it in other contexts. Eventually, try using some of the words yourself. Ask a proficient friend or a friendly teacher to check that your usage is correct, clear, and appropriate.

And **use a dictionary intensively** for further reinforcement. A good dictionary will tell you how words are used in different situations. Buy and use a mid-sized hardcover college dictionary such as the ones listed below. It will give you guidance on typical uses, combinations with other words, and shades of meaning. Some of these dictionaries are meant especially to guide people learning English as a new language.

SECOND LANGUAGE

- ***Collins Cobuild English Dictionary***. London: HarperCollins, 1995.
- ***Concise Oxford Dictionary***, 7th ed. Oxford: Clarendon, 1982.
- ***Funk and Wagnall's Canadian College Dictionary***. Toronto: Fitzhenry and Whiteside, 1989.
- ***Gage Canadian Dictionary***, revised. Toronto: Macmillan, 1996. Toronto: Gage, 1996.

- ***ITP Nelson Canadian Dictionary of the English Language***. Toronto: Nelson, 1996.
- ***Merriam-Webster's Collegiate Dictionary***. 10th ed. Markham, Ontario: Allen, 1993.
- ***Oxford Advanced Learner's Dictionary of Current English***. 4th ed. Oxford: Oxford University Press, 1989.

Note: **Dictionaries in CD-ROM** form (often combined with a thesaurus) are a great convenience, allowing you to look up words while you're writing and making it easy to browse among related words. Be aware, though, that you may get only simplified definitions and almost no guidance on usage.

PRACTICAL TIP

Using the Dictionary Profitably

Say you're trying to finish up a problem set in Chemistry and also getting ready for an Anthropology test the next day. One problem involves a dye with an *affinity* for wool fabrics, apparently meaning that it combines with them easily, but you've been reading about *affinal relatives* as if they're less close than blood relatives. And what does any of this have to do with the flyer for an *affinity credit card* that your university has just sent?

If you were to use the word yourself, would it be affinity *to, with, for,* or *between*? And (in case you get called on to outline your answer in Chem tutorial) how do you pronounce the word?

Your dictionary will throw light on all these angles. Here's the section from *Merriam-Webster's Collegiate® Dictionary*, 10th ed. © 1993. (By permission from Merriam-Webster Inc.)

af·fil·i·at·ed \-lē-ˌā-təd\ *adj* (1795) **:** closely associated with another typically in a dependent or subordinate position ⟨the university and its ~ medical school⟩

¹af·fine \a-ˈfīn, ə-\ *n* [MF *affin*, fr. L *affinis*, fr. *affinis* related] (ca. 1509) **:** a relative by marriage

²affine *adj* [L *affinis*, adj.] (1918) **:** of, relating to, or being a transformation (as a translation, a rotation, or a uniform stretching) that carries straight lines into straight lines and parallel lines into parallel lines but may alter distance between points and angles between lines ⟨~ geometry⟩ — **af·fine·ly** *adv*

af·fined \a-ˈfīnd, ə-\ *adj* (1597) **1 :** joined in a close relationship **:** CONNECTED **2 :** bound by obligation

af·fin·i·ty \ə-ˈfi-nə-tē\ *n, pl* **-ties** [ME *affinite*, fr. MF or L; MF *afinité*, fr. L *affinitas*, fr. *affinis* bordering on, related by marriage, fr. *ad-* + *finis* end, border] (14c) **1 :** relationship by marriage **2 a :** sympathy marked by community of interest **:** KINSHIP **b** (1) **:** an attraction to or liking for something ⟨people with an ~ to darkness —Mark Twain⟩ ⟨pork and fennel have a natural ~ for each other —Abby Mandel⟩ (2) **:** an attractive force between substances or particles that causes them to enter into and remain in chemical combination **c :** a person esp. of the opposite sex having a particular attraction for one **3 a :** likeness based on relationship or causal connection ⟨found an ~ between the teller of a tale and the craftsman —Mary McCarthy⟩ ⟨this investigation, with *affinities* to a case history, a psychoanalysis, a detective story —Oliver Sachs⟩ **b :** a relation between biological groups involving resemblance in structural plan and indicating a common origin ***syn*** see ATTRACTION

affinity chromatography *n* (1970) **:** chromatography in which a macromolecule (as a protein) is isolated and purified by passing it in solution through a column treated with a substance having a ligand for which the macromolecule has an affinity that causes it to be retained on the column

affinity group *n* (1970) **:** a group of people having a common interest or goal or acting together for a specific purpose (as for a chartered tour)

af·firm \ə-ˈfərm\ *vb* [ME *affermen*, fr. MF *afermer*, fr. L *affirmare*, fr. *ad-* + *firmare* to make firm, fr. *firmus* firm — more at FIRM] *vt* (14c) **1 a :** VALIDATE, CONFIRM **b :** to state positively **2 :** to assert (as a judg-

cont'd

PRACTICAL TIP

- The derivation involves borders, and the first (or main) meaning is "related by marriage." So even though the technical term *affinal* isn't listed here, those *affinal* relatives now make sense. And you could turn to the capitalized word KINSHIP to get an explanation of the distinction.
- The second meaning of "sympathy" and "liking" seems a bit personal for the dye, but the specialized meaning **2 b (2)** eventually shows the specific meaning in terms of chemistry. Here the preposition is definitely *between*, though *to* and *for* both show up in other examples.
- The *affinity card* might refer to that idea of liking, or maybe to your "common origin" as members of the same university. And the entry for *affinity group* just down the list confirms that the use of the word to mean a group with a common interest came into the language just before 1970.
- You can pronounce *affinity* the way it looks, putting most stress on the second syllable, which sounds like the "fin" of a fish. If you have to answer orally in Anthropology, though, the entries for *affine* and *affined* warn you that related words sometimes sound more like "find." (The key to pronunciation symbols inside the back cover of the dictionary shows how to use markings like these.)

PRACTICAL TIP

Using the Thesaurus Safely

Use the **thesaurus** with caution. A thesaurus can remind you of words you already know, but it's dangerous if you rely on it to make your vocabulary seem larger. A thesaurus sets out groups of words with roughly the same meaning—but *roughly* isn't good enough when you care about the effects on your reader. Academic readers care deeply about exact meanings in the vocabularies of their discipline and will be annoyed rather than impressed by words used even a little wrongly—especially fancy or pretentious words.

Don't ever accept a computer thesaurus list of synonyms as an adequate definition either—you'd sound pretty foolish in Chemistry if you accepted "similarity" as a meaning for *affinity*, for instance.

If you decide to consult a thesaurus, whether in book or computer form, keep a good dictionary at hand to check the exact meaning, usage, and level of formality of words you're considering.

Choosing Unbiased Language

Recent social changes have made people aware of the ways wording elevates some groups of people and downgrades others. Here are some ways to keep your language free of unintentional bias.*

Prefer Gender-Neutral Forms

Many standard wordings seem to assume that every individual is male. Instead of inserting *his or her* each time, you can often just use plural forms.

* Two handbooks for further guidance on these points are Casey Miller and Kate Swift, *The Handbook of Nonsexist Writing*, 2nd ed. (New York: Harper, 1988) and *Guidelines for Bias-Free Writing* (Bloomington: Indiana University Press, 1995).

Seems to exclude women	**Man** is a tool-building animal.
Inclusive	**Humans** are tool-building animals.
Seems to exclude women	Each artist must find **his** own way to represent his vision.
Inclusive but awkward	Each artist must find **his or her** own way to represent **his or her** vision.
Inclusive	**Artists** must find **their** own ways to represent **their** visions.

Note: The use of plural *they* or *their* to refer to a singular noun (e.g., *artist*) is technically incorrect, but common in speech and increasingly acceptable in formal prose when it helps avoid gender-biased language. Use it, however, only when one of the previous patterns is impossible.

See People as Individuals

Don't refer to people merely as representatives of categories. Avoid using adjectives as collective nouns: the arthritic, blondes, etc. "Blonde-haired people"or "people with arthritis" are easy-enough substitutes.

Use special terms when they recognize useful distinctions. A *hearing-impaired* person has some hearing, for instance, while a *profoundly deaf* person has none. But *vertically challenged* to mean *short* is just silly. If the characteristic is important enough to mention, give the exact height to be more precise.

Some terms have outlived their usefulness. For example, it's more precise as well as more considerate to note that a person has Down's syndrome rather than saying that he's dumb or an idiot. Ethnic and racial terms are especially delicate. Follow what is currently most acceptable to the person or people you are discussing.

Deal Fairly with Dated Quotations

Historical or literary texts follow the customs of their own times, not of ours. Sometimes you can just paraphrase instead of quoting exact words. Or you can put your paraphrase alongside a quotation to show your interpretation of its idea. Comment on the wording only if you are sure the original meaning was distorted. The use of [*sic*] to draw attention to old-fashioned wording is misleading.

Obtrusive	Pope forgot women when he said, "The proper study of mankind [*sic*] is man [*sic*]."
More subtle	Pope affirmed the need for human self-awareness when he said, "The proper study of mankind is man."

Avoid Gendered Labels

It is seldom useful to assign labels on the basis of sex roles, especially to single out women as if they were exceptions. Feminine forms of occupational titles (such as *poetess* or *woman doctor* or *policewoman* or *chairwoman*) are objectionable because they suggest that a woman in the role of poet or doctor or police officer is not the real thing. Just use the non-gendered forms such as *poet, doctor, police officer, chair*.

Titles like *Mr., Mrs.,* and even the recently invented *Ms.* are less and less used orally in most parts of North America, and their place in writing is limited. They are still expected in the salutations of letters (*Dear Ms. Singh, Dear Professor Savoie*). If you don't know the person's sex, just omit the title and write the whole name (*Dear Jean Chrétien, Dear Vannevar Bush*).

In academic essays, reviews, and reports, use only last names when you refer to your sources. Omit titles, even *Professor* and *Doctor*. When your essay concentrates on a specific figure, you may want to give the full name on first mention, then revert to last name only.

✓ Emily Dickinson published only three poems in her lifetime.... Dickinson is now considered a major American poet.

Getting the Details Right

Small elements of wording can make the difference between a distracted reader and a satisfied one. (But don't let that idea stop you from writing a draft at full speed. You can always polish later.) The advice in this section is for use in the editing stage. If English is your native language, you won't need to work on all of the points here.

Articles

The little words *a* and *the*, which are called **articles**, send subtle signals about the nouns that follow them. They don't cause problems for people who have spoken English since childhood, but are puzzling for those learning English later in life. When you need guidance in choosing between *a* and *the*, start by going through the following sequence of questions and then see where your noun fits on the chart.

1. Is the Noun Uncountable or Countable?

Don't use *a* with uncountable nouns. Remember that *a* (*an* before vowels) is really the numeral *one*. In English, words referring to masses, fluids, and collections of items (*applesauce, water, equipment*) can't be counted or made plural. Abstract ideas (such as *love, justice, success, knowledge*) also cannot be made plural or counted.

Note: Some words can be **either uncountable or countable**, depending on whether they are referring to a **specific** item (countable) or **generically** to a sort of item (uncountable).

Generic (uncountable)	*Specific (countable)*
I like to eat **chicken**.	Don't count your **chickens** before they're hatched.
I went to **school** in Germany.	I attended **a school** for children of NATO personnel. **The school** was located on the army base in Sollingen.
She strove for **success**.	Her novel was **a great success**. She was surprised by **the sudden success** of her novel.

As language develops, more and more nouns are used as countable. We now say *a democracy* and count *the democracies* in Asia; we even order *a whisky* and take *an aspirin* afterwards. In these cases we are assuming that the reader understands that we are referring to a unit (really *a democratic country, a drink of whisky, a tablet of aspirin*).

2. Is the Noun Indefinite or Definite?

- If an item is one example of a category, use the **indefinite article**, *a* (or *an*).
- If you mean all the items in the category, use no article.
- When you want to point to a specific item or items, use the **definite article**, *the*.
- If you specify just which item you mean (perhaps by using a clause starting with *who, which,* or *that*), use the definite article, *the*.
- If the readers know just which item you mean (perhaps because you have mentioned it before), use the definite article, *the*.

The following table will get you through most cases. There are a number of exceptions, but with time, you will be able to trust your ear to get most articles right.

ARTICLES: CHOOSING THE RIGHT ONE

	Indefinite **(*a* or no article)**	**Definite** **(*the*)**
Singular:		
Uncountable	Give me liberty or give me death. All you need is love. He supplied valuable information.	**The** death of Stalin led to **the** release of many prisoners. Having **the** right equipment is essential to **the** task. She attends **the** University of Calgary.
Countable	**An** archeologist must work hard. It is **a** museum's task to entertain.	**The** eminent archeologist Walter Kenyon worked at **the** Royal Ontario Museum.
Plural:		
Countable	They shoot horses, don't they?	He painted **the** horses and **the** gentlemen of **the** eighteenth-century landed class.
	Writers need readers.	**The** writers of **the** prize-winning novels will meet **the** readers who judged them.

Note: You have a choice about article use when you want to refer to an item as typical or representative of its class: you can say either *a sonnet, the sonnet,* or *sonnets*.

Prepositions

These little words are a challenge if you're learning English as a second language. A few have logical meanings indicating physical relationships (*against, beside, over, through*), but the most common ones (*to, at, in, on*) take practice to pick up. Use the chart below to reinforce what you hear in everyday speech and notice in your reading.

When you are writing an important document, you will find it worthwhile to use a dictionary for checking specific usages. Look up the noun or verb for which you need a preposition and check the entry for guidance. (See the dictionary entry quoted on page 136 for an example.)

Time	
in [a time of day]	in the morning, in the afternoon, in the evening
in [a specific month or year]	in May, in December, in 1997
at [a specific clock time]	at nine o'clock, at noon, at 10:23 a.m., at five o'clock in the morning
on [a specific day]	on Wednesday, on Wednesday 2 May, on Labour Day
Place	
in [a specific named location]	in New York, in England, in Sloane school, in the house
at [a generic location]	at university, at school, at home, at the lake
to [direction]	to New York, to work, to school, to the city

Means

with [a specific instrument]	with a pencil, with a compass, with a computer
by [by more general means]	by good luck, by working hard, by air

Focus

about [less formal]	speak about, talk about, chat about
on [more formal]	talk on, speak on, lecture on

PRACTICAL TIP

Ending a Sentence with a Preposition

Don't worry much about the old "rule" that you shouldn't end a sentence with a preposition. It's true that you can insert *which* or *whom* and reorganize the sentence, putting the preposition in the middle, but that usage now sounds very formal. The British prime minister Winston Churchill parodied it when someone criticized him for breaking the rule. "That is the kind of pedantry," he said, "up with which I will not put."

Gerund or Infinitive?

Another challenge, especially for second-language speakers, is knowing when to use the *-ing* forms of verbs. It is confusing to hear people say *I like **going*** but never *I want **going***, and to hear both *I like **swimming*** and *I like **to swim***. Some words take only the gerund or only the infinitive, others take either, according to intended meaning. As with prepositions and articles, build up your "ear" by listening and reading with attention to this detail. For important passages—perhaps for the introductory and concluding paragraphs of assignments—you may need to check your choices by reading through a dictionary entry about the "controlling verb." (If you're wondering whether to write "pretended to die" or "pretended dying," for instance, read through to the end of the entry about *pretend*.)

The patterns set out below may also provide some shortcuts. The chart outlines some of the distinctions made unconsciously by native speakers, showing how the choice between infinitive and gerund can determine shades of meaning. Keep it in mind as you draft, and use it to confirm hard choices.

Infinitive (with to*)*	*Gerund (*-ing*)*
for intended, tentative, uncompleted, actions	*for actual, vivid, completed actions*
I like to go	I like going
[NOT USED: I avoid to go]	I avoid going
I must remember to go	I remember going
I fell overboard, so I tried to swim	I needed exercise, so I tried swimming

Spelling Without Tears

Remembering their childhood struggles to write documents by hand, many people are worried about spelling. It's true that wrongly spelled words bother readers, and can even lead to misunderstandings. But when you write on a computer, help is readily available. A **spell checker** contains a list of correctly spelled words. When you have typed something that's not in the list, your computer will let you know and suggest alternatives. Thus, it will also catch many typing errors as well as spelling errors.

What's more, the spell checker is also the quickest way to adjust to new ways of spelling English words if you have moved from one national spelling system to another. Set the dictionary to the Canadian version and you won't have to wonder whether it's *honour* or *honor*, *analyze* or *analyse*, for instance.

Here are some tips on making the best use of computerized spell checking:

- Let it be part of the editing rather than the drafting stage. Instead of being interrupted constantly by beeps, finish writing a section and then run it through the checker. Do that repeatedly during your drafting.
- Don't let the checker change words automatically. Use your own judgement to see if the suggested word makes sense in the sentence. Pull out your print dictionary if you need further guidance.
- Spell checkers don't recognize the names of people and places, nor do they know technical terms. Check these words yourself against a printed document you trust, working a few letters at a time. Then to avoid repeated bother, use the "Add" button to put these words into the checker's list.

There will still be a few frequent spellings—of key terms in a course, for instance—that you need to learn by memory, especially for writing exams. Write them out by hand a number of times to reinforce your sense of how they look, sound, and even feel to write. Analyze their structure to reinforce your knowledge. (See pages 134–135 on learning new vocabulary words.)

Sorting Out Confusable or Misused Words

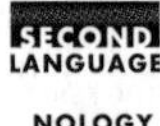

English is rich in words that sound or look similar but have distinct meanings. Computer **style checkers** can give some warnings about them, but the responsibility is still on you to sort them out. The following list sets out some common problem points for student writers. Use the wide margins to write in other pairs or trios that cause you trouble.

accept/except

The verb *to accept* means "to receive willingly or favourably." The preposition *except* means "excluding," and the verb *to except* means "to exclude."

✓ The electorate **accepted** the promises of the politician.

✓ She passed all her courses **except** Philosophy.

✓ The law **excepts** farmers from the regulation about slow-moving vehicles.

advice/advise

Advice is a noun; *advise* is a verb. You *advise* someone and you seek *advice* from someone.

✓ I **advise** you to seek the **advice** of a lawyer.

affect/effect

As a verb *to affect* means "to influence"; as a noun *affect* is a technical term in Psychology, meaning "the display of a feeling or emotion."

✓ Caffeine **affects** the nerves.

✓ The subjects showed various degrees of **affect** in their response to hearing another infant's cry. [*technical*]

Effect is occasionally used as a verb, meaning "to cause to occur." As a noun, *effect* means result.

✓ The dean intends **to effect** certain changes in the curriculum.

✓ The **effect** of lowered taxes is diminished social programs.

alot/a lot/allot

The spelling *alot* is incorrect for the two-word phrase *a lot*—which in any case is too colloquial for most academic writing. Don't let a spell checker tell you to substitute the verb *allot*, meaning "to distribute."

✓ As a civil servant, he could **allot** contracts to **a lot** of his friends.

allusion/illusion

An *allusion* is an indirect reference, whereas an *illusion* is a deception or faulty perception.

- ✓ Much poetry communicates by **allusion** to things not mentioned explicitly.
- ✓ The **illusion** of a quick profit tempted the speculators.

among/between

Use *among* for more than two, *between* for two.

- ✓ The three victors split the conquered land **among** themselves.
- ✓ Please keep this secret **between** you and me.

amount/number

Use *amount* when you are talking about uncountable quantities; use *number* for countable items. (See page 141 on countable and uncountable nouns.)

- ✓ The **amount** of water in the reservoir fell during the drought.
- ✓ The **number** of migrating Canada geese has decreased as a result of global warming.

can/may/might

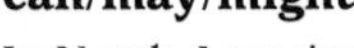

In North America, *can* and *may* are used interchangeably.

British writers make a distinction. They use *can* to mean "be able," and *may* to refer to permission. In another sense, *may* also indicates future possibility; *might* indicates a less likely possibility.

- ✓ By the age of eight, most children **can** cross the street by themselves.
- ✓ The schoolchildren **may** not cross the street by themselves; they are required to wait for a crossing guard.
- ✓ New learners **may** take years to gain confidence.
- ✓ They think they **might** never learn.

capital/capitol

The noun *capital* is used to indicate great importance; it may mean "a seat of government," "the top of a pillar," "an uppercase letter," or "accumulated wealth." A *capitol* is a particular North American or ancient Roman legislative building.

- ✓ The **capital** expenditures for the new company were over three million dollars.
- ✓ The **Capitol** is a landmark in Washington, D.C.

complement/compliment

Whether as a noun or verb, *complement* means “completion” or “to complete.” *Compliment* means “praise” or “to praise,” also as either a noun or a verb.

- ✓ Her writing skills **complemented** her oral skills.
- ✓ Not wishing to offend any of the contest entrants, Zak **complimented** them all on their culinary talents.

council/counsel

The noun *council* refers to an advisory, deliberative, or administrative body of people who meet regularly. As a noun, *counsel* means “advice” or “advisor” (sometimes specifically a lawyer); as a verb, it means *to advise.*

- ✓ The student **council** unanimously voted to abolish hazing week.
- ✓ The school psychologist **counselled** both students and instructors during the crisis.

criterion/criteria

Criterion (a principle or standard for comparison) is a singular noun. *Criteria* is its plural.

data/datum

Data is the plural form of the noun *datum*. Although *data* is commonly used as a singular noun, this usage is still not acceptable in formal writing. Use a plural verb with *data*.

- ✓ The **data** for the experiment were lost when the computer system failed.

disinterested/uninterested

Disinterested means “impartial, not standing to profit”; *uninterested* is the word that means “not interested.”

✓ Perkins, not having invested in the company, was a **disinterested** judge.

✓ Lalonde, though he had invested in the company, was **uninterested** in its daily transactions.

good/well

Good is an adjective. *Well* can function as either an adjective meaning "effectively" or an adverb meaning "healthy."

✗ My friends know that I did **good**.

✓ Jason plays the piano **well**, and he is also a **good** goalie.

✓ The patient felt **well** enough to resume work.

imply/infer

To imply means to strongly suggest. *To infer* means to conclude from facts and reasoning.

✓ The tone of the discussion **implies** that the subject is not important.

✓ The investigation used circumstantial evidence to **infer** guilt.

its/it's

Its is a possessive pronoun. Like all personal pronouns, it uses no apostrophe to form the possessive. *It's* is a contraction of *it is* or *it has*.

✗ **Its** about time to visit the library.

✓ **It's** about time to visit the library.

✓ **It's** been a long time since the beginning of term.

lead/led

The verb *lead* changes both pronunciation and spelling to form the past tense.

✓ She will **lead** the party to victory.

✓ She had **led** the party to victory.

less/fewer

Use *less* with uncountable nouns, such as money and water. Use *fewer* with countable nouns. (See page 141 on the distinction.)

- ✓ The experiment showed that infants display **less** emotion when their mothers are absent.
- ✓ The experiment showed that **fewer** infants cried when their mothers were present.

lie/lay

To lie means to rest in a horizontal position; *lay* is its past tense. *To lay* means to place or set down; *laid* is its past tense.

- ✓ The tired children should **lie** down for a nap. Yesterday they **lay** in bed for two hours.
- ✓ The crown prosecutor **lays** charges in criminal cases. Yesterday she **laid** a murder charge.

literally/figuratively

Literally means "exactly as stated"—it does not mean "figuratively," or "metaphorically."

- ✗ I am **literally** dead with exhaustion after spending a full day in classes.
- ✓ Smoking can **literally** coat the airways with tar residue.

media/medium

Media is the plural form of the singular noun *medium*.

- ✓ Reports about the trial appeared in three news **media**: radio, television, and newspapers.
- ✓ Radio was the only **medium** of mass communication in the country.

phenomena/phenomenon

Phenomenon is the singular form and *phenomena* is the plural form of this word, which refers to something unusual or extraordinary that can be seen or heard with the senses.

- ✓ The earth's moon was once considered a unique **phenomenon**, but modern astronomers have shown that other planets also have moons.
- ✓ The Perseid showers are yearly **phenomena**, displaying thousands of meteors in the August night sky.

principal/principle

Used as an adjective, *principal* means "first in importance" or "main." As a noun, *principal* means the head of a school. The noun *principle* is a law used as the basis for reasoning.

✓ The feast is the **principal** event of the ritual.

✓ The **principal** of the school led the students in welcoming the foreign exchange students.

✓ The **principle** of relativity transformed twentieth-century physics.

rational/rationale

The adjective *rational* means *logical*. The noun *rationale* means the logical reasoning or basis of something.

✓ Spock always makes **rational** decisions.

✓ Black's **rationale** for dismantling the pension plan did not convince the employees.

their/there/they're

Their is a possessive, third-person pronoun, meaning "of them." *There* means "at a particular point or place"; it can also be used as an introductory word in a sentence or clause, though it tends to make for wordy phrasing. *They're* is a contraction of *they are*, so it is unlikely to be used in academic writing.

✓ **Their** relationship was doomed.

✓ **There** the story ends.

✓ In most fairy tales, **there** is a clearing at the edge of the woods.

✓ **They're** not going to get away with it.

your/you're

Your is used to show possession; *you're* is a contraction of *you are*—and contractions are seldom suitable for academic papers.

✓ **You're** going to miss **your** family when you move to England.

CHAPTER 9

PUNCTUATION AND OTHER CONVENTIONS: Guiding Your Reader

Punctuation can be a powerful tool. Though hardly noticeable to readers, it guides them from one thought to another and creates emphasis for specific ideas. Those dots and squiggles make up a system of signals that help give written texts some of the intonations and pauses of speech. Each punctuation mark has its own meaning, but there is often a choice among "correct" marks, depending on the rhythm and emphasis you want to create.

This chapter will outline the principles underlying the most common uses of punctuation, and it will review problem points that students face. If you don't know which mark you need, start with this list of functions, and follow up by reading the relevant entry or entries for further guidance:

- ***Marking sentence boundaries and joins*** period, semicolon, colon, dash, comma *(with coordinating conjunction)*
- ***Adding ideas*** comma *(after introductory element, before final modifier),* parentheses, dash, quotation marks
- ***Allowing interruptions*** commas *(paired),* dashes *(paired),* parentheses, brackets
- ***Indicating relationships*** colon, comma *(for non-restrictive elements),* apostrophe, hyphen
- ***Indicating importance*** capitals, italics/underlining/bold
- ***Indicating omissions*** period, apostrophe, ellipsis

The Period /./

The period is the most emphatic mark of completion. Because it's such a simple mark to print, it is also used to signal commonly used short forms.

1. Use a period at the end of a sentence. (See page 120 for a reminder of what makes a sentence complete.) Orally, you would run sentences together. In formal writing use a period to mark off the separate units:

   ✓ Heads I win, tails you lose. [in speech and informal writing]

   ✓ Heads I win. Tails you lose. [in formal writing]

2. When you paraphrase a question rather than quoting it directly, end your sentence with a period, not a question mark:

   ✗ The referendum asked whether voters wanted Quebec to open negotiations for independence?

   ✓ The referendum asked whether voters wanted Quebec to open negotiations for independence.

3. Use a period after conventional abbreviations for titles, place names, scientific names, terms of measurement, and acronyms.

   The period signifies that letters have been omitted from a word. British writers omit the period if the last letter of the word is intact (*Mr* for "Mister," but *Gen.* for "General"), whereas North American writers maintain it for such titles. Most writers in all countries often omit periods in common short forms for places and units of measurement:

North American	Mr. Chrétien	British	Mr Major
North American	Dr. King	British	Dr Thatcher

British Columbia = BC	Massachusetts = MA
United States = US	United Kingdom = UK
millilitre = mL	inch = in. [*period to avoid ambiguity*]
ampere = A	angstrom = Å

Acronyms—words formed from initial letters—generally don't contain periods. Some have become part of the language, functioning as words. Only in extremely formal prose, such as a legal document, would you need to substitute the long forms for common acronyms like these:

AIDS = acquired immune deficiency syndrome

laser = light amplification by stimulated emission of radiation

ROM = read-only memory

IQ = intelligence quotient

Latin initials and abbreviations, on the other hand, always take periods. In most student writing, however, it's clearer just to use the English equivalent.

e.g. = *exempli gratia* = for example

i.e. = *id est* = that is

etc. = *et cetera* = and so on

vs. = *versus* = against

PRACTICAL TIP

Getting Abbreviations Right

A good dictionary will give you the standard abbreviations for full words, and it will give you the full forms for standard abbreviations and most acronyms too if you look them up as words.

PRACTICAL TIP

Spelling Out Abbreviations and Acronyms

Not all readers will recognize an abbreviation or acronym on its first appearance. It is wise to write out the full form of the term the first time you use it, giving the abbreviation or acronym in parentheses immediately following. Then you can continue using the short form, knowing that your readers have just had a review lesson on its meaning.

The Semicolon /;/

A semicolon creates a less abrupt break between main clauses than a period. The elements on either side of a semicolon must be equal in grammatical form—two full sentences, or two equivalent items in a list.

1. Use a semicolon to **join two sentences** closely connected in thought. The second clause restates the idea of the first or contrasts with it:

   ✓ Some rebels took the penalty meekly; others refused to comply with the court order.

   Sometimes a conjunctive adverb (*however, moreover, nevertheless, therefore, additionally, in fact, for example*) helps indicate the relationship between the two sentences. Check that the second part is a complete sentence:

✗ Sales were good, however, expenses continued to be high.

✓ Sales were good; however, expenses continued to be high.

✗ Watercolour paints consist of a mixture of dry pigment, water, and an adhering gum; in addition, honey or glycerin to slow drying time.

✓ Watercolour paints consist of a mixture of dry pigment, water, and an adhering gum; in addition, honey or glycerin may be included to slow drying time.

2. Use a semicolon to **divide off units in a list** if one or more units contain commas (it's not necessary otherwise):

   ✓ Xenophon wrote several works, including *Hellenica*, a Greek history of the period from 411 to 362 B.C.E.; *Agesilaus,* a eulogy of the Spartan King; and *Cypropaedia,* a novel in which Cyrus I appears as the model ruler.

The Colon /:/

The colon, like the semicolon, is a less abrupt stop than the period. Unlike the semicolon, it can join items of unequal grammatical type, often leading from a general statement to an explanation or set of examples. It gives a sense of expectancy: something interesting is coming.

1. Use a colon to **introduce a list**, whether the list is printed horizontally or vertically. (Lists of five items or more are usually printed as indented columns.) Make sure your sentence is complete before introducing the list.

   ✓ A university consists of four main parts: property, administrative staff, teaching faculty, and students.

   ✓ The procedure requires the following equipment:

   1 roll of gauze and some adhesive tape
   4 wax pencils
   4 sterile lancets
   24 cotton balls
   1 bottle of rubbing alcohol

Note: The colon should not separate a linking verb (forms of *to be, to seem, to become,* etc.) from the rest of a sentence:

✗ The gifts of the Magi were: gold, frankincense, and myrrh.

✓ The gifts of the Magi were gold, frankincense, and myrrh.

✓ The gifts of the Magi were exotic luxuries of the time: gold, frankincense, and myrrh.

2. Use a colon **between two sentences** when the second one gives a specification, explanation or example for the first. Used sparingly in formal prose, this construction sets up a satisfying pattern of promise and fulfillment:

   ✓ The United Nations failed in its mission for one reason: it did not react strongly.

   ✓ The fatality rate among patients infected with lassa fever is high: the virus kills cells faster than the body can defend itself.

3. Use a colon **to introduce a long quotation** or to announce an emphatic short quotation. Again, complete your own sentence before using the colon:

   ✓ Hamlet put it best: "To be or not to be."

   ✓ Conway compares overly nurturant teaching to permissive child-rearing: "Both obfuscate the nature of power and thus limit the possibility of rebellion."

   However, you may use a comma rather than a colon to introduce a short quotation less formally:

   ✓ As Churchill noted, "Westward lay the march of American Empire."

The Comma /,/

The comma represents a pause and often a change of intonation in your sentence, and thus helps set up the rhythm and emphasis you want. Sometimes you can rely on your ear to place commas, but the following guidelines will help you make logical choices.

1. Use a comma along with a coordinating conjunction (*and, or, nor, for, but, yet*) to join two sentences while also showing that they contain two ideas. If the grammatical subject of both sentences is the same entity, you may omit the comma:

   ✓ Hard work may create wealth, **but** family connections also help. [the two grammatical subjects are *work* and *connections*]

   ✓ Hard work may create wealth **but** not result in happiness. [*work* is the grammatical subject of both clauses]

2. Use a comma to mark off non-restrictive elements from the rest of a sentence. (A non-restrictive element is one that is not strictly needed for understanding the sentence, though it may add useful or interesting information.) It can be just a few words or a whole clause (usually starting with *who* or *which*).

   Note: Check that you have used a comma on each side of the non-restrictive element. Many people use the first one but forget the second.

   ✓ Maurice Penney, **Vice-President of Planning,** delivered the opening speech.

   ✓ The students, **who have studied hard,** are having a winter break.

   ✓ Students **who have studied hard** will pass the exam. [*compare—here the same words with no commas around them give the meaning "**only** those students who have studied hard will pass the exam"*]

3. Use a comma before adding an additional (non-restrictive) element at the end of the sentence, whether it is a subordinate clause or just a few words expanding on a previous idea:

   ✓ This method is becoming increasingly common, especially outside North America.

   ✓ Napoleon insisted that his troops continue the march into Russia, a doomed effort.

   ✓ Napoleon insisted that his troops continue the march into Russia, although his generals warned him that the tactic was doomed to failure.

PRACTICAL TIP

Choosing Between *That* and *Which*

If you see that you have used the word *that* in a relative clause, you probably intend a restrictive clause, needing no commas. Check by seeing if you can name a specific logical relationship between the ideas in the clause and those in the rest of the sentence. Another check is to listen to your voice as you read the sentence out loud. If your tone dips to a lower note for the relative clause, you probably intend a non-restrictive clause, requiring *which* and commas.

> ✓ **The areas that have been clearcut no longer have fish.** [*implies that the two ideas are causally related*]
>
> ✓ **The remoter areas, which are strikingly scenic, no longer have fish.** [*suggests no specific relation between the two ideas*]

4. Use commas to mark both sides of interrupting words and phrases:

   ✓ Napoleon, however, insisted that his troops continue the march into Russia.

   ✓ George Eliot, as her readers soon discovered, was a woman.

5. Use a comma after an introductory phrase when omitting it would cause confusion:

   ✗ In the sky above the stars twinkled.

   ✓ In the sky above, the stars twinkled.

6. Mark off items in a list with commas. You can choose whether to omit the comma before the final *and*—but leaving it in creates a more emphatic effect:

   ✓ Hobbes said that human life in a state of nature was solitary, poor, nasty, brutish, and short.

   ✓ A standard essay has an introduction, a body and a conclusion.

   Exception: Don't use a comma when you set out *pairs* of words or ideas.

✓ Hobbes stressed that human life in a state of nature was brutish and short.

✓ The essay must both introduce your arguments and sum up your conclusions.

Exception: Don't use a comma when adjectives pair up to modify a noun that follows them:

✓ The delegates enjoyed a pleasant summer barbecue.

Test that pattern by seeing whether you can reverse the adjectives. If you lose the intended meaning, then omit the comma. (Here *summer pleasant barbecue* does not make sense.)

7. Use a comma to divide off elements in addresses and dates:

✓ 162 Forest Lane, Edmonton, Alberta

✓ A huge deposit of nickel in Sudbury, Ontario, was probably caused by the impact of a meteorite.

✓ Wednesday, January 1, 1997

Exception: The metric system of day/month/year omits commas. This method is becoming increasingly common, especially outside North America:

✓ Wednesday 1 January 1997

The Dash /—/

The dash signifies an interruption, giving the effect of energy and impetus, as if the writer were rushing on to give the next point. In informal prose, it can substitute occasionally for periods, colons, semicolons, and even some commas and parentheses. But overuse of dashes can make writing seem disjointed.

Note: You can type two hyphens together to serve as a dash, or use a special typographic character from your computer "Insert" menu. It's not necessary to have spaces on either side.

- ✓ Heads I win—tails I lose. [*instead of a period or semicolon*]
- ✓ They missed India but found a continent instead—America. [*instead of a colon*]
- ✓ We need to gain further donors—preferably rich ones. [*instead of a comma*]
- ✓ In 1954 Marilyn Bell—only sixteen years old—swam across Lake Ontario. [*instead of parentheses*]

The Exclamation Mark /!/

Use the exclamation mark in informal writing or dialogue to indicate excitement. It is rarely used in the sober world of academic writing.

- ✓ I hate Mondays!
- ✓ Proofread your work!
- ✓ The phrase Americans did not want to hear became a byword for emergency: "The Russians are coming! The Russians are coming!"

Quotation Marks /" " or ' '/

American writers use double quotation marks, while British writers use single quotation marks. In Canada and other British-influenced countries, either practice is acceptable, but the trend is strongly towards using double quotation marks (as we do in this book).

1. Use quotation marks to report conversation:
   - ✓ The next step is a leading question such as "Why don't you take the car for a test drive?"

   For a quote within a quote, use the opposite kind of quotation marks from your primary style (single or double marks):

   - ✓ Gloucester resolves to bear affliction "till it do cry out itself 'Enough, enough.'"

2. Use either quotation marks or italics to single out a particular word or phrase as the focus of attention. To show the translation of a word, use italics for the foreign word and quotation marks for the English one.

   ✓ The battle cry "Power to the people" recurs in American history.

   ✓ The term "hegemony" has become fashionable.

   ✓ The word *agape* is sometimes translated as "love."

   Quotation marks can also set off an unconventional usage of a word or phrase, such as a slang word that you want for special effect. Use this signal sparingly, however, or the reader will get the sense that you don't stand behind your own choice of words.

   ✗ He was a "troubled" child and a "psychotic" adult.

   ✓ He was thought of as a "troubled" child, and he developed into a psychotic adult.

3. Use quotation marks when you cite the titles of poems, short stories, songs, films, journal articles, and book chapters. They signify that the work you are mentioning is part of a larger unit. (Titles of books, films, paintings, symphonies, and operas should be italicized.)

   ✓ Coleridge's poem "The Rime of the Ancient Mariner" was first published in the 1798 collection *Lyrical Ballads*.

Placement of Punctuation with Quotation Marks

North American and British practices differ in the placement of final punctuation for quotations. British writers always put it outside the punctuation marks. The following instructions show the usual practice in the United States and Canada.

1. Place a comma or period **inside** quotation marks, even where the period or comma was not part of the original words:

   ✓ American "The bicycle freed women from restrictive, conventional dress," a popular historian asserts, "by bringing forth the then-startling bloomer costumes."

2. Place a semicolon or colon **outside** quotation marks:

   ✓ Concertgoing used to mean listening to "Fugue in G Minor"; in the 1960s, however, it came to mean experiencing the Beatles' "A Hard Day's Night."

3. Place a question mark or exclamation mark **inside** quotation marks if it is part of the quotation. Place these items **outside** the quotation marks if they are not part of the quotation.

   ✓ Jason asked, "What does an A+ essay look like?"

   ✓ Did he believe her comment that "this is an A+ essay"?

4. Parentheses for a reference go **outside** the quotation marks and **before** the remaining punctuation:

   ✓ "If anything became apparent during 1994, it was that no one could seem to agree on what the information highway was" (Broadhead 6).

The Apostrophe /'/

The apostrophe shows the relationship of ownership or possession. It also indicates omitted letters in some short forms. These are the basic patterns:

1. To show possession, add apostrophe and *s* to:

   - All singular and plural nouns that do not end in *s*:

     ✓ a cat's nine lives

     ✓ the men's lavatory

     ✓ Yeltsin's speech

   For the sake of clear pronunciation, singular nouns that already end in ***s*** usually take an apostrophe and *s* like other singular nouns, ending up with *s's*:

     ✓ the boss's newspaper

     ✓ Ross's testimony

Historical names ending in *s*, however, usually don't take this extra *s*:

✓ Moses' leadership (*or* the leadership of Moses)

✓ Socrates' trial (*or* the trial of Socrates)

- Indefinite pronouns:

✓ someone's graffiti

✓ one's temperament

✓ anybody's guess

Exception: Do not use the apostrophe to make possessive forms for personal pronouns—they change form instead. Note especially the form *its*.

I ➜ **mine**	we ➜ **ours**
you ➜ **yours**	you ➜ **yours**
he ➜ **his**	
she ➜ **hers**	they ➜ **theirs**
it ➜ **its**	

2. To show possession, add an apostrophe alone to plural nouns ending in *s*:

✓ families' cars

✓ the Smiths' house

✓ storms' centres

✓ the two Darwins' legacy

Choosing Between *It's* and *Its*

PRACTICAL TIP

It's is the contraction for *it is* (*It's raining*) or *it has* (*It's been a hectic day*). You will hardly ever use it in academic writing. What's more, there is no such word as *its'*. So get used to seeing *its* as a common and correct form meaning "belonging to it."

3. In informal writing, use an apostrophe in contractions to mark the place of missing letters. Avoid contractions in formal academic writing.

Informal	*Formal*
summer of '94	summer of 1994
can't	cannot
I'm	I am
it's	it is *or* it has

Parentheses /()/

Parentheses signify interruption. They make a less emphatic interruption than dashes, but a more distinct interruption than commas.

1. Place parentheses around an explanation, example, or qualification that is incidental to the main idea of a sentence:

   ✓ Giocondo (the only son of nine children) spent his formative years learning his father's trade.

   ✓ John George Diefenbaker was the thirteenth prime minister of Canada (1957-1963).

   As in the last of the preceding examples, put the sentence's punctuation **after** the closing parenthesis. But if the words inside the parentheses form a complete sentence in themselves, put the period inside the parentheses.

   ✓ The customer began wearing his wristwatch on December 26. (It was a Christmas gift.) By January 6, it was no longer operating.

2. Use parentheses around citations, placing any punctuation **after** them. (See pages 35–53 on other elements of citation format.)

   ✓ Coleridge also used the word *vital* to mean something "mysteriously significant" (Hulme 65).

   ✓ Another study found that infants show responsive crying when they hear the taperecorded cry of another infant (Sammon, 1997).

Brackets /[]/

Brackets are square to distinguish them from parentheses, which are round. They mark the interruption of your text by external information.

1. Use brackets around words of your own inserted in a quotation:

   ✓ According to Schneider (1997), "The washing machine did not liberate women [from domestic chores], but it did improve sanitation."

2. Use brackets to enclose the Latin word *sic*, which means "thus." *Sic* is used to show an apparent error in the quotation (always italicize it):

   ✓ She asserts that Marie Antoinette quipped, "Let them eat cakes [*sic*]."

The Hyphen /-/

Hyphens show joins inside words or between words.

1. You may use a hyphen to divide a word at the end of a line, though you should avoid it whenever possible. Usually you can rely on the automatic hyphenation of your wordprocessing program, but sometimes it is necessary to divide words manually, for example to improve the appearance of a narrow newspaper-style column. When manually hyphenating, follow these guidelines:

   - Don't divide words of one syllable
   - Don't leave one letter by itself
   - Divide between syllables according to dictionary entries, which show the syllabic structures of each word. You will find that prefixes are always kept together, as are most suffixes, and that double consonants are usually divided (*pre-po-si-tion, con-sti-tu-tion-al, stop-ping*).

2. Use hyphens to create compound words out of separate single words:
   - ✓ horse-breeding practices
   - ✓ twentieth-century ideas
   - ✓ mother-in-law

Words that used to be joined by a hyphen are increasingly spelled as two words or one:

barber-shop quartet	barbershop quartet
book-binder	book binder *or* bookbinder

3. Use a hyphen to attach certain prefixes (*all-*, *anti-*, *co-*, *ex-*, *pre-*, *post-*, *pro-* and *self-*) to existing words. (You will notice that some of these hyphens get dropped as the words become common parts of the language.)

✓ ex-husband		✓ anti-imperialism
✓ post-colonial	*but*	✓ postoperative
✓ co-owner	*but*	✓ cooperate

4. Use hyphens to emphasize contrasting prefixes, even when the first one is left "hanging." Type a space after the first prefix as if it were a word in itself:
   - ✓ The two armies behaved in the same way both **pre-** and **post-treaty**.

PRACTICAL TIP

Testing for Hyphens

You will see certain word groups sometimes with hyphens and sometimes without. Word groups functioning as adjectives need hyphens only when they come before the noun they modify. *Test:* If you pronounce the set of words by stressing one main syllable, you have a compound adjective—use a hyphen.

✓ Our house is full of nineteenth-century furniture.

but

✓ Our house is full of furniture built in the nineteenth century.

5. Use a hyphen to separate compound numbers from one to a hundred, and fractions used as modifiers.

✓ three hundred ninety-five

✓ three-year-old children *but* ✓ The children are three years old.

✓ the one-quarter line *but* ✓ The price is reduced by one quarter.

6. Use a hyphen to indicate *to* and *from* in a pair of numbers:

✓ 1965-1995 ✓ pages 5-20

The Ellipsis /.../

An ellipsis is typed as a set of three spaced periods. It replaces a word, phrase, sentence, or paragraph that you want to omit from a quotation, indicating that your sentence does not fully repeat the original text.

(*Note:* The remaining words should still form a complete sentence—and reflect the author's meaning accurately.)

Within a sentence, use three periods, placing a space before and after each one:

✓ "Life insurance is . . . the most important of all financial arrangements," says *The Wealthy Barber*.

To show an omission after a completed sentence, use four periods, with no space before the first.

✓ Pauk (1993) refers to studies showing that exercise "decreases stress and anxiety. . . . raises self-esteem and well-being and decreases depression" (page 23).

Exception: Do not begin or end a quotation with an ellipsis—the quotation marks are enough to signal that you have omitted something beforehand and afterwards.

✗ Hamlet's hypersensitivity is shown in his inner debate about whether ". . . to be . . ." or not.

✓ Hamlet's hypersensitivity is shown in his inner debate about whether "to be" or not.

Italics, Boldface, and Underlining

Italics are *slanted letters like this* that give special status to a word. (If you use a printer that cannot produce high-quality italics, underline the text instead.) Now that high-quality printers are common, **boldface** sometimes replaces italics or <u>underlining</u> because it is more distinct and easier to read, but most writers try to use boldface for special purposes only (as in this book).

1. Italics can mark the titles of books, plays, films, long poems that are complete books, and lengthy musical pieces.
    - ✓ *Out of Africa* is one of my favourite movies.
    - ✓ *Paradise Lost* is Milton's most famous poem.
2. Italics can emphasize an idea. However, use this device sparingly. See pages 107–108 on other ways to achieve emphasis.
    - ✓ Please hand in exams *immediately*.
3. Italics, like quotation marks, can emphasize a word as a word. To give a translation, use italics for the foreign word and quotation marks for the English word.
    - ✓ Although the poet repeats the words *true love*, he never fully reveals what he means by the term.
    - ✓ In French, the word *pain* means "bread."
4. Italics identify foreign words or expressions:
    - ✓ The judge wanted to address us *in camera*.
    - ✓ The males of *Drosophila melanogaster* perform an elaborate courtship display.

Capitals

Capitals add emphasis. That's why a capital letter signals the start of a sentence and is used for proper names. You can print the title of your paper in **FULL CAPITALS**. For any text longer than eight or ten words, though, experts generally agree that a mix of upper- and lowercase letters is easier to read. You might choose full capitals for the main title, but mixed case for other headings.

1. Capitalize the first letter of proper names: that is, names and titles of specific people, nationalities, geographical places, academic subjects, months, days of the week, and commercial brands. Note that some words are uncapitalized when they have a general meaning, but take a capital when they become specific:

✓ Dr. Alison Sills		✓ West Haven, Connecticut
✓ Tuesday 17 March		✓ United Nations
✓ Wednesday		✓ Kleenex
✓ Mother Teresa	*but*	✓ my mother
✓ Queen Elizabeth	*but*	✓ a queen bee
✓ the rise of the West [*a distinctive region*]	*but*	✓ a view to the west [*a direction*]
✓ the Chemistry exam		✓ the chemistry of cooking

The Latin names of plants and animals follow a standard pattern to help show the levels of classification:

✓ *Eschirichia coli* [*E. coli* after the first use]

✓ *Drosophila melanogaster* [*D. melanogaster* after the first use]

For titles or headings that mix capitals and lowercase letters, capitalize the first letter of each word except articles (*a, an, the*) and short prepositions (*at, of, from, in, to* **but** *After, Between, Except*)

Other Conventional Symbols

Many other marks besides letters can stand for words. Here are some guidelines for their use in student writing.

Numerals

In general, it is suitable to spell out numbers under twenty and use numerals for the rest.

Use numerals rather than words when you specify the unit of measurement and when you use a decimal or percent sign.

✓ 5 cm ✓ 15 litres

✓ $20 ✓ 22%

Don't start a sentence with a numeral. Sometimes you can change the word order to avoid it.

✗ 8 men came.

✓ Eight men came.

If you need to use two numbers together as modifiers, spell out one and use a numeral for the other.

✓ ten 4-way stop signs ✓ the first 12 people

Printed Symbols

Many other marks create the printed equivalents of words. They are indispensable for calculations and handy for tables, but not all are suitable for use in prose. Here are some basic guidelines to keep in mind for your academic papers and reports. To check usage of more technical symbols such as Greek letters and mathematical signs, note the way they are handled in your readings and consult specialized handbooks for your discipline.

SYMBOL	NAME	MEANING	USAGE
@	*at* sign	*at*	In e-mail addresses and price lists. Otherwise, spell out.
&	ampersand	*and*	Between authors' names in APA-style parenthetical references. Spell out in essays, reports, and letters.
*	asterisk, star	[emphasis, attention]	To signal the importance of a specific item in a list, or to direct the reader to a footnote in informal writing.
¢, $, £	cents, dollars, pounds	[denominations of money in some countries]	For any reference to a specific amount of money. Spell out only as name of currency (*The buyer paid in American dollars*).
#	number sign	*number*	Spell out *number* in your text. In labelling illustrations, just give the numeral (*Table 3, Figure 2*).
/	forward slash	[signals a sequence or alternatives]	Used as a separator in a hierarchy of computer file directories; means "or" in logical phrases such as *and/or*. Otherwise spell out.
%	percent sign	*percent*	With specific numbers in lists, tables, and charts. Otherwise, spell out. (Always spell out the word *percentage*.)
<, >	*less than, greater than* signs	*less than, greater than*	Only for calculations, formulas, and tables and charts. Otherwise, spell out.

INDEX